Youth Justice:
Challenges to Practice

Martin Stephenson
and Rob Allen

unitas
EngageCreateAchieve

First published 2012 by Unitas

Unitas
Eastgate Place
Salhouse Road
Norwich
NR13 6LA

Unitas is a charity registered in England and Wales. Charity No. 1133286
Registered Office: 10 Queen Street Place, London, ECAR 1BE, UK
www.unitas.uk.net

The paper used in this publication is procured from forests independently certified to the level of Forest Stewardship Council® (FSC®) principles and criteria. Chain of custody certification allows the tracing of this paper back to specific forest-management units (see www.fsc.org).

ISBN:978-1-907538-99-5

About the authors

Martin Stephenson is currently Executive Director of Unitas. He was a member of the Youth Justice Board from1998 to 2002. His youth justice publications include *Young People and Offending: Education, Youth Justice and Social Inclusion* (Willan 2007), Effective *Practice in Youth Justice* with Sally Brown and Henri Giller (Willan 2011) and various reports for the Youth Justice Board such as the *Audit Of Education And Training Provision Within The Youth Justice System* (2001).

Rob Allen is an independent researcher and consultant specialising in youth justice and prisons. He is the co-founder of Justice and Prisons (www.justiceandprisons.org). From 2005 to 2010, Rob was Director of the International Centre for Prison Studies at King's College London and he was a member of the Youth Justice Board from 1998 to 2006.

Roger Hopkins Burke is Principal Lecturer and Criminology Subject Leader at Nottingham Trent University, where he teaches criminological theory and young people, crime and justice to both undergraduates and postgraduates. His numerous publications include *Zero Tolerance Policing* (Perpetuity Press 1998), *Hard Cop, Soft Cop* (Willan 2004), *Young People, Crime and Justice* (Willan 2008), *An Introduction to Criminological Theory* (Willan 2001, 2005, 2009, 2013 forthcoming) and *Criminal Justice Theory: An Introduction* (Routledge 2011).

Maggie Blyth is currently Independent Chair of Kent Safeguarding Children Board. Prior to this she held similar roles in Nottingham, Central Bedfordshire and Herefordshire. She is also a Member of the Parole Board for England and Wales and a Member of the UK Health Professions Council. With a background as a senior manager in the Probation Service during the 1990s, Maggie set up the first Youth Offending Service in Oxfordshire in 1999, and between 2001 and 2005 she was a senior policy advisor at the Youth Justice Board for England and Wales. She has published on children at risk, including a recent analysis of the Munro Review.

Heidi Dix has been a social worker since 1997 and has worked in both adult and children's services. Since 2007 she has worked as a Senior Officer in Suffolk Youth Offending Service, where she has facilitated the development of effective, evidence-based practice. Heidi is also a lecturer in social work at University Campus Suffolk, where she teaches law and social policy. Her interests include single gender work, participatory ways of engaging young people within the youth justice system and exploring a relationship-based approach within effective practice.

Jennifer Meade is County Performance Manager at Suffolk Youth Offending Service. Prior to this, she introduced the Drug Interventions Programme in Norfolk, and worked as a senior probation officer in Nottinghamshire and probation officer in Derbyshire, and as volunteer manager at The Landmark, a centre for people living with HIV and AIDS. She has a long-standing interest in the role of case management and the client–worker relationship in effective practice. She is also interested in how best to bridge the divide between policy, research and practice.

Contents

Introduction

Rob Allen and Martin Stephenson

This book is primarily designed to augment *Effective Practice in Youth Justice* (Stephenson, Giller and Brown 2011). It provides a range of perspectives that aim to stimulate managers and practitioners to think about how best they can use research evidence to support their practice with young people.

With the UK facing a prolonged period of austerity, police, YOTs and custodial establishments are all being required to 'do more with less'. Effective practice becomes all the more crucial in this context. Only with the necessary knowledge, skills and professional judgement will practitioners be able to identify the best way of working with the individual cases, families or neighbourhoods that comprise their workload.

The government's decision to retain the Youth Justice Board (YJB) should help ensure the continuation of a more coherent policy-making focus in Whitehall on youth crime and young offenders. But for practitioners, effective practice has always involved making sense of the myriad ways in which the state relates to young people and their families. Where young people live, the education, training and employment available to them, the ways they use their leisure time all have an impact on their prospects. So, as well as direct face-to-face work with children and young people, effective practice necessarily involves working with other agencies, advocating for young people and helping to ensure that comprehensive measures are in place that give the best chance of a positive outcome.

The chapters here on safeguarding, custody and desistance all emphasise the need, in various ways, for work beyond one-to-one casework. To set the scene for consideration of these specific topics, the book opens with a chapter that provides a broad examination of the link between theory and practice.

One of the accusations of the 'what works' approach — at least in its narrow sense — is that it is ostensibly atheoretical. It focuses simply on those interventions that have been validated by the highest research standards, irrespective of underlying theory, and this apparent pragmatism has attracted politicians and policymakers. From another perspective, those youth justice managers who see the world in binary terms, of 'thinking' and 'doing' as separate activities, might query the relevance of any theory compared to the 'reality' of practice. Of course, just as the closely allied what works and risk-management approaches are underpinned by certain theoretical or at least ideological assumptions (Smith 2007), so too is the work of all managers and practitioners, whether this is made explicit or not. These theories may sometimes be no more than distant memories of primary training, based on outcomes of a particular case or simply following fads and fashions (Trinder and Reynolds 2000). Particular practice models are, to a greater or lesser extent, grounded in a theoretical framework. Similarly, most of the research findings that influence practitioners are derived from testing aspects of particular theories.

For practitioners, operating within a well-thought-through and consistent explanatory framework about why young people offend and what can be done to address and prevent it can be an important aid to clear, defensible and consistent decision-making. Arguably, practitioners in the 1980s and 1990s, for example, benefited from working within a clear framework based on labelling theory, which put a premium on diversion from criminal justice processes and minimising interventions with those who had already entered the system. But defining success in terms of diverting young people from prosecution, keeping sentences as low down the tariff as possible and avoiding custodial remands and sentences at all cost sometimes meant a greater focus on managing the system and its decisions rather than addressing the needs of young people. From the late 1990s, the emphasis changed, with greater priority attached to positively tackling offending behaviour by young people, the development of multi-agency working in the form of YOTs, and a range of tools such as *Asset* and KEEP produced by the YJB. However, it is probably the case that youth justice practitioners often make little use of research or theory in their day-to-day work (Trotter 1999) and that they rely more on sources of knowledge such as accumulated life experience, which could be termed practice wisdom.

Accordingly, Roger Hopkins Burke's chapter is essential reading. Hopkins Burke helpfully condenses the potentially confusing array of theories to explain crime by young people in terms of three models: the rational actor model; the predestined actor model, encompassing theories such as those dealing with cognitive learning, altered biology and deviant subcultures; and the victimised actor model, which includes labelling, conflict and radical theories among others. He emphasises that these categories are not mutually exclusive and that comprehensive, effective intervention in the life of a young person in the youth justice system almost certainly requires an eclectic approach drawing on all three.

Safeguarding is an interesting topic in that it did not figure among the YJB's effective practice priorities and was never enshrined in a KEEP, seen instead as part of the *Asset* assessment process. The reason for this may be partly due to the dearth of evidence on the effectiveness of different child protection procedures – self-evidently, randomised controlled trials could hardly be conducted to examine their effectiveness. Critics might also argue that it also reflects the youth justice model introduced in 1998, with its emphasis on deeds rather than needs. Similarly, the risk-management approach tends to focus on risk to others rather than to the young people themselves. Maggie Blyth in 'Troubled or troublesome. Safeguarding children in the youth justice system: custody and community' points out that there is evidence that young people in the youth justice system suffer a double jeopardy: not only are they disproportionately at risk of abuse in its different forms but this also tends to be significantly underestimated by practitioners. Blyth urges greater integration of the work of YOTs and the child protection planning system through monitoring and using the Common Assessment Framework (CAF) at all times paying great attention to the views and experience of children and young people. Her chapter also underlines one of the key messages of the recent Munro review: frontline staff should move from a risk-averse to risk-sensible practice and exercise of their professional judgement should be recognised and encouraged.

Nevertheless as Blyth points out adolescents are a relatively high-risk group in relation to fatalities; 132 young people died in serious incidents while under supervision in the community between 2006 and 2011. The failure to learn from SCRs is being tackled through the requirement for LSCBs to devise a learning and knowledge framework, including a systematic method of learning from cases. In fact, the criticisms that Munro levied in her review of the child protection system – that professionals have become constrained by the demands and rigidity of current systems and quality has been more about compliance with procedures than a focus on learning – echoes criticisms of the youth justice system since 1998. Both child protection and youth justice are accused of displacing relationship-building, innovation and reflection through an over-emphasis on regulations, procedures, targets and audits. In the context of safeguarding, youth justice practice may have two further weaknesses in that the range of risk behaviours a young person may be involved in could lead practitioners to normalise the perception of risk in the young person's life. Second, the focus on the young person and their actions may lead to less work with those who may potentially be harming them through neglect or maltreatment.

The numbers and treatment of young people imprisoned tends to reveal a society's attitude towards young people more generally. Rob Allen's chapter, 'Custody and resettlement', should be read in conjunction with the 'Custody and resettlement' chapter in *Effective Practice in Youth Justice*. It uses the latest evidence on trends in the use of custody and inspection to examine critically ways of reducing numbers in custody and the quality of practice in secure establishments.

Although only a tiny proportion of young people in the youth justice system experience custody, they represent some of the most vulnerable young people in our society and are a testimony to serial failure by many of our agencies. Despite the very significant costs of custody and the recent substantial fall in numbers, some secure establishments fail to cater for even basic needs, such as ensuring that young people feel safe, have appropriate contact with their families, are well fed and have daily access to showers. While shortcomings in the basic environment are more likely to prevent rather than promote attitudinal change, more direct attempts to change attitudes and behaviour have also had disappointing results. Two key weaknesses in intervention are identified: the inconsistent and ineffective implementation of the personal officer role and poor co-ordination of assessment and care planning.

Rob Allen's practice priorities for those working in custody are to ensure that custodial care meets the basic needs of all and the specific needs of particular groups before applying more ambitious programme interventions. Second, he recommends adopting an approach in line with the messages from desistance studies rather than from the what works perspective with its emphasis on particular programmes or modes of intervention.

Advocating a 'desistance paradigm' for custodial practitioners, where there is a focus on opportunities and motivation so that young people can develop their capacity to resist and overcome pressures to return to crime, Allen highlights work with families and community integration processes. He also puts forward the idea that elements of compliance or procedural justice theory, which argue that compliance with justice agencies is crucially dependent on transparent fairness, is particularly applicable to secure settings. For practitioners in the community, Allen identifies the following priorities: a high-level of diversion from court; an effective tariff management strategy; appropriate bail intervention programmes; and avoidance and management of breach.

Given that prevention of reoffending is the primary goal of all work with young people in the youth justice system, as defined by the 1998 Crime and Disorder Act, then as Martin Stephenson's chapter highlights, desistance is a surprisingly neglected research topic. Much of the theoretical work has addressed the reasons for the onset of crime and research has centred on the effectiveness of particular programmes or interventions. The approach to the implementation of accredited programmes or simplistic what works guidance has been criticised for neglecting the importance of effective relationships (McNeill and Batchelor 2002; Tilley 2006). Desistance studies attempt to answer the questions of 'how', 'why' and in 'what circumstances' the processes of ceasing offending occur. The evidence, though far from conclusive, indicates that the quality of the relationship between young people and practitioners in the youth justice system may be a significant element in desistance. A desistance paradigm broadens the relatively narrow conception of effectiveness under a what works approach and puts more emphasis on the skills and knowledge of practitioners who work with young people in the youth justice system.

The experiences and insights of young people are crucial to understanding the process of desistance and these are reflected in interview material drawn from the large-scale Summer Arts College (SAC) programme, in which nearly half of all YOTs have participated (Tarling and Adams 2012).

One of the key challenges for youth justice organisations and for individual practitioners within them is how to embed 'effective practice' within service delivery. Dix and Meade's chapter describes how one youth offending service (referred to as County Youth Offending Service or CYOS) set about doing this. From a starting point where there were no systems in place to judge the quality of work and no real sense of 'what good looked like', the authors outline a systematic approach to change based on belief in a fundamental blend of skills, knowledge and experience that practitioners bring to their work. Central to this, they argue, is the capacity of practitioners to form empathetic, respectful 'working alliances' with young people in which there is agreement about the nature and purpose of what needs to be achieved through intervention.

This requires, the authors suggest, curiosity and interest on the part of practitioners, within a learning culture in which creativity and risk taking are encouraged and supported. The approaches outlined in this chapter therefore focus on how services can foster and develop inquisitiveness and 'research mindedness' in practitioners, giving them greater autonomy to lead on innovations as 'champions of effective practice' supported within a systematic 'innovation process'. They conclude that building a culture in which change can happen requires that practitioners should not feel constrained by a culture of evidence-based practice, but instead feel inspired to develop as critical, reflective thinkers.

Several common messages emerge from these contributions: the skills and knowledge of practitioners are crucial in bringing about positive change; the views and experiences of young people are vital in encouraging their engagement and helping them bring about positive changes; and practice is as much as about influencing the external environment of a young person as concentrating on subjective change.

References

McNeill F and Batchelor S (2002) 'Chaos, containment and change: responding to persistent offending by young people', *Youth Justice*, 2: 1.

Smith R (2007) *Youth Justice: Ideas, Policy, Practice* (2nd edn). Cullompton: Willan.

Stephenson M, Giller H and Brown S (2011) *Effective Practice in Youth Justice* (2nd edn). Abingdon: Routledge

Tarling R and Adams M (2012) *Summer Arts Colleges: Digest of the Evaluation Report*. London: Unitas.

Tilley N (2006) 'Knowing and doing: guidance and good practice in crime prevention', *Crime Prevention Studies*, 20: 217–252.

Trinder L and Reynolds S (eds) (2000) *Evidence-based Practice: A Critical Appraisal*. Oxford: Blackwell Science.

1
Theories of criminology and youth justice

Roger Hopkins Burke

Introduction

This chapter explores how different criminological theories explain juvenile offending behaviour and why it is that some offenders come to desist from criminal involvement. In this necessary brief résumé of a complex and extensive area of research, three models of offending behaviour are considered. First, the *rational actor model* proposes that juveniles enjoy free will and that involvement in crime is simply a matter of choice. By contrast, the *predestined actor model* advises that criminality can be explained by factors, internal or external to the individual, which cause or determine them to act in ways over which they have little or no control. Third, the *victimised actor model* proposes that offenders are themselves victims of an unequal and unjust society where the choices they make are invariably restricted by the socially excluded circumstances in which they live. The chapter demonstrates that these models are not mutually exclusive and that a comprehensive intervention in the life of the individual young offender requires consideration of all three (Hopkins Burke 2008).

Rational actor model

The purist variant of the rational actor model has its origins in the 18th century and proposes that criminal behaviour is the outcome of rational, calculating individuals exercising free will and choosing to commit crime in preference to involvement in law-abiding activities. The recommended criminal justice response is that offenders should be held fully responsible for offences they commit and be punished accordingly. Since the calculus for making the choice to offend is the acquisition of a benefit (pleasure), society must develop policies to increase the cost of this benefit (pain). Thus punishment should become incrementally harsher as the extent and impact of criminal behaviour becomes greater and more serious, while the costs of crime must always outweigh the possible benefits that might be obtained.

Fixed punishments for all offences must be written into the law and not be open to the interpretation, or discretion, of judges, while crucially the law must be applied equally to all citizens, with the sole function of the court being to determine guilt. There should be no mitigation. All found guilty of a particular offence should suffer the same prescribed penalty. The punishment should fit the crime and not the characteristics and/or circumstances of the individual.

Table 1: Rational actor model

▶ Humans are rational beings who enjoy free will

▶ People choose to engage in criminal behaviour

▶ Society must punish criminals to deter individual wrongdoers and other would-be criminals

▶ Punishment should be proportional to the offence committed

▶ Punishment must be guaranteed and delivered quickly.

(Adapted from Hopkins Burke 2008: 88)

The purist rational actor model proposition is an appealing but nevertheless flawed argument. Children, the 'feeble minded' and the insane were all treated as if they were fully rational and competent but it became increasingly apparent that this was clearly not the case. The outcome was a compromise where ordinary, sane adults were considered to be fully responsible for their actions but others – children in particular – were considered less responsible for their actions. Subsequent revisions to the penal code thus admitted to the courts for the first time non-legal 'experts', including doctors, psychiatrists and later social workers, to determine the extent to which offenders were responsible for their actions. The outcome was that sentences became more individualised and dependent on the perceived degree of culpability of the offender. Furthermore, it was recognised that particular punishments would have different effects on different people. Consequently, punishment came increasingly to be expressed in terms of the individual characteristics of the person and their potential for rehabilitation.

The rational actor model went into increasing decline as an explanation of offending behaviour but returned to favour during the last quarter of the 20th century when rising crime levels were blamed on weakening sources of social authority, the family, schools, religion and other key institutions, and on the corrosive influence of the surrounding legitimating culture, with its emphasis on rights rather than responsibilities. It was once again proposed that offenders should take responsibility for their actions and that punishment was to be about devising penalties to fit the crime and ensuring they were carried out (Hopkins Burke 2009).

Contemporary rational actor theories

There are three groups of contemporary rational actor model theories: a) contemporary deterrence theories; b) contemporary rational actor theories; c) routine activity theories.

Contemporary deterrence theories

These are founded on the twin rational actor principles that punishment must occur quickly after the offence has been committed and it certainly must be carried out. If the punishment is sufficiently severe, certain to occur and swift, the rational individual will conclude that there is more to be lost than gained from offending (Wright 1993). There are two variants of the deterrence doctrine and these operate in different ways. With *general* deterrence the apprehension and punishment of offenders demonstrates clearly to all what will happen if they break the law, while *specific* deterrence demonstrates to the apprehended and punished individual the futility of criminal involvement. However, the high rate of recidivism challenges the effectiveness of deterrence as a crime control strategy, with reoffending rates for juveniles leaving custody historically high (Hopkins Burke 2008).

Contemporary rational choice theories

Contemporary rational actor theories originally compared the decision-making process of offenders with straightforward economic choice. The person chooses the activity – either legal or illegal – that offers the best return and, it is argued, could be deterred by a more effective and rigorous criminal justice system (Becker 1968). Not surprisingly, this early version was accused of implying too high a degree of rationality, particularly in the case of juveniles. Clarke and Cornish responded with an influential modified variant where they defined crime as 'the outcome of the offender's choices or decisions, however hasty or ill-considered these might be' (Clarke 1987: 118). Offenders would thus not always obtain all the facts needed to make a wise decision, and the information available would not necessarily be weighed carefully or appropriately, but they would make a decision that was rational in the context of their lives, experiences, cultural background and knowledge base. A juvenile brought up in a location where criminality is common, with their family and friends actively involved in illicit activities that appear to bring them easily obtained material rewards, and where access to legitimate opportunities appear both limited and implausible, could well consider criminal involvement a very rational choice.

Routine activities theory

Routine activities theory proposes that, for a crime to occur, there must be at the same time and place a perpetrator, a victim and/or an object of property (Felson 1998). The offence can take place if there are persons or circumstances in the locality that encourage it to happen but it can be prevented if the potential victim or another person present take action to deter it. Cohen and Felson (1979) argued that fundamental changes in daily activities related to work, school and leisure that had occurred during the past 50 years had placed more people in particular localities at certain times and increased their accessibility as crime targets while they were away from home and unable to guard their own property and possessions.

It is often juveniles who are to be found wandering the streets when adults are at work and who are prepared to take advantage of crime opportunities when they arise. And this is most likely when they are in the company of likeminded others, in particular when they are truanting or excluded from school, or in subsequent years when, having left school with inadequate educational qualifications, they find themselves excluded from legitimate economic opportunities.

Rational actor model: conclusions and policy implications

This model proposes that juveniles *choose* to offend because it makes rational sense to them in the context of their lives. Offending choices are more attractive than legitimate activities, which are usually unavailable to them or of limited value. Deterrence theory suggests that juveniles can be deterred from criminality by the threat or imposition of rigorous penalties but recidivism rates suggest that this strategy has not been very successful. The other strategy implication is to improve the life chances of the juvenile so they have access to good quality, legitimate opportunities that make offending a less rational choice. Offenders will desist from criminal behaviour when they are provided with such rational alternatives.

Predestined actor model

The predestined actor model replaces the rational actor notion of free will with the doctrine of determinism, where offending is explained in terms of factors, internal or external to the individual, which cause them to act in ways over which they have little or no control. There are three basic formulations of this model – biological, psychological and sociological – but all incorporate the same fundamental assumptions.

Table 2: Predestined actor model

❱ The rational actor emphasis on free will is replaced with the doctrine of determinism

❱ Criminal behaviour is explained in terms of factors, internal or external to the individual, that cause people to act in ways over which they have little or no control

❱ The individual is thus in some way predestined to be a criminal

❱ There are three basic formulations of the model – biological, psychological and sociological – but all incorporate the same fundamental determinist assumptions

❱ Treatment of the offender is proposed rather than punishment.

(Adapted from Hopkins Burke 2008: 98)

Biological theories

Biological theories have their origins in the work of the Italian school at the end of the 19th century. Lombroso (1875) famously argued that criminals are a physical type distinct from non-criminals. While his work is considered simplistic by the standards of today, he later importantly recognised the need for multifactor accounts that include hereditary, social, cultural and economic factors. Ferri (1895) also argued that criminal behaviour could be explained by studying the interaction between physical, individual and social factors, proposing that crime could be controlled by improving the living conditions of the poor. It is a key tenet of purist predestined actor model philosophy that some form of treatment should be used to correct the behaviour of the offender.

Biological theories were to become increasingly more sophisticated but invariably remained problematic. The notion of inherited criminal characteristics was a central theme, although research ultimately failed to distinguish between biological and environmental factors (see Hopkins Burke 2008, 2009). *Genetic structure* explanations considered abnormalities in the genetic structure of the offender. Thus some men were found to have an extra female chromosome (with supposedly more female characteristics) while others had an extra male chromosome (supra-male characteristics). Nevertheless, these theories were flawed, not least because it was found that there were thousands of perfectly normal and harmless people in the general population with an extra chromosome. The more recent discovery that some traits of personality can be explained by a genetic component (Jones 1993), however, does strengthen the possibility that *some* criminal behaviour can be explained by an inherited genetic *susceptibility*, which is triggered by environmental factors.

Criminal body type theories proposed that offenders are organically inferior people, with Sheldon (1949) linking different types of physique to temperament, intelligence and criminality and Glueck and Glueck (1950) proposing that offenders have different shaped bodies than non-offenders. Problematically, all these researchers failed to establish whether juveniles were offenders because of their build and disposition, because their physique and dispositions were socially conceived as associated with offenders, or whether poverty and deprivation affected both their body build and offending behaviour.

Biochemical theories link criminality with substances that are either already present in the body of the individual or are created by some internal physiological process. It has long been recognised that most male animals are more aggressive than females and this has been linked to the male sex hormone, testosterone, although the relationship between the two in human beings appears more ambiguous. Olwens (1987) nevertheless found a clear link between testosterone and verbal and physical aggression in young males, with a further distinction between provoked and unprovoked aggressive behaviour. Schalling (1987) found high testosterone levels in young males to be associated with verbal but not actual physical aggression, which suggests a concern to protect their status by threats. Ellis and Crontz (1990) observed that testosterone levels peak during puberty and the early 20s, which correlates with the highest crime rates, although they produced no real evidence of a causal relationship.

Hypoglycaemia or low blood sugar levels may result in irritable, aggressive reactions and *may* culminate in sexual offences, assaults and motiveless murder. Shoenthaler (1982) discovered that by lowering the daily sucrose intake of incarcerated juveniles it is possible to reduce the level of their antisocial behaviour, while Virkkunen (1987) linked hypoglycaemia with truancy, low verbal IQ, tattooing and stealing from home during childhood.

Baldwin (1990) proposed that the significant link between (young) age and crime rates can be partially explained by arousal rates, observing that juveniles quickly became used to stimuli that had previously excited them and sought ever more thrilling inputs. The stimulus (or buzz) received from offending was found to decline with age, as did the level of physical fitness, strength and agility required to perform many of these activities.

Altered biological state theories connect behavioural changes in the individual with the introduction of an external chemical agent, and establish links between irritability and aggression that may lead individuals to commit criminal assault. Research on the criminological implications of allergies to such things as pollen, inhalants, drugs and food suggests two main reactions: emotional immaturity, characterised by temper tantrums, screaming episodes, whining and impatience, and antisocial behaviour characterised by sulkiness and cruelty (Virkkunen 1987).

Substance abuse occurs through the intake of drugs, some legal and freely available, such as alcohol, glues and lighter fluids, others prescribed by the medical profession, such as barbiturates, and those only available illegally, such as cannabis, amphetamines, LSD, MDA or ecstasy, and opiates (usually cocaine or heroin). Alcohol is extremely significant because it is readily available and long been associated with antisocial behaviour and crime.

Alcohol and young people are closely linked in the public mind but this has not always been the case. In the interwar period, young people were the lightest drinkers in the adult population and alcohol did not play a significant part in the youth culture that emerged during the 1950s. It was not until the 1960s that pubs and drinking became an integral part of the youth scene; by the 1980s, those aged 18 to 24 years had become the heaviest drinkers in the population. Hazardous drinking is now most prevalent in teenagers and young adults: 32 per cent of females between 16 and 19 years of age and 62 per cent of males between 20 and 24 have a hazardous drinking pattern. These changes have been accompanied by a decline in the age of regular drinking, with many drinking regularly by the age of 14 or 15 (Institute of Alcohol Studies 2005). There is also a growing trend of drinking for effect and intoxication, which is partly related to the merging of the alcohol and drug scenes in youth culture. Alcohol is now one of a range of psychoactive products available on the recreational drug market in the UK. A large survey of teenagers found that, by the age of 15 or 16, binge drinking was common, as was being 'seriously drunk' (Jefferis, Power and Manor 2005).

The term alcohol-related crime usually refers to offences involving a) a combination of criminal damage, drunk and disorderly and other public disorder offences; b) young males, typically 18 to 30; and c) the entertainment areas of town and city centres. Research shows that a high proportion of victims of violent crime are drinking or under the influence of alcohol at the time of their assault and a minimum of one in five people arrested by police test positive for alcohol (Bennett 2000).

Widespread illegal drug use has emerged in the UK since the late 1960s. Drugs are chemicals that alter the biochemical balance of the body and brain and can affect behaviour in different ways depending on the type and quantity of the drug taken. The biological effects of cannabis and opiates such as heroin tend to reduce aggressive hostile tendencies, while cocaine and its derivative crack are more closely associated with violence. The most commonly used drug by young people is cannabis, which has been used by 33 per cent of young men and 22 per cent of young women. Ecstasy is the most commonly used class A drug, with higher use among 16 to 24 year olds, while in recent years there has been an increase in the use of cocaine among young people, especially among males. By contrast, the use of amphetamines and LSD has declined (Institute of Alcohol Studies 2005). Drug use has been found to be widespread among school pupils, although there has been a decrease in prevalence in recent years (Department of Health 2005).

In summary, a number of biological studies suggest that some individuals are born with a physiological condition that predisposes them to commit crime but closer investigation suggests that social and environmental background is at least equally important. Evidence nevertheless suggests that, in cases where the biology of the individual has been altered through the introduction of a foreign chemical agent such as diet, alcohol and/ or illegal drugs, behaviour can be substantially changed and criminal involvement may follow.

There have been attempts in recent years to rehabilitate biological explanations by incorporating social and environmental factors into a 'multifactor' approach. These sociobiologists argue that the presence of certain biological predispositions – and the introduction of foreign chemical agents – may increase the likelihood, but not determine absolutely, that an individual will offend (Mednick, Moffit and Stack 1987). Jeffery (1977) observed that poor people are more likely to experience a poor quality diet and to be exposed to pollutants, with the resulting nutrients and chemicals transformed by the biochemical system into neurochemical compounds in the brain. Poverty thus leads to behavioural differences, which occur through the interaction of the individual and environment.

Wilson and Herrnstein (1985) argued that an amalgam of gender, age, intelligence, body type and personality factors constitute the individual, who is projected into a social world where they learn what kind of behaviour is rewarded in which circumstances. Heavily influenced by psychological behaviourism (see below), the authors argued that individuals learn to respond to situations according to how their behaviour has been previously rewarded and punished, and their environment should therefore be changed in order to produce the kind of conduct desired. Thus, in order to understand the propensity to commit crime, it is important to identify the ways in which the environment might operate on particular individuals to produce this response. Within this general learning framework, the influence of the family, school and wider community is identified as being crucial.

Psychological theories

Psychological theories direct our intention to notions of the 'criminal mind' or 'personality', where it is proposed that there are patterns of reasoning and behaviour specific to offenders and that these remain constant regardless of different social experiences. There are three broad categories of psychological theories. While the first two – *psychodynamic* and *behavioural learning theories* – have firm roots in the predestined actor tradition, the third – *cognitive learning theories* – reject much of the positivist tradition and, in incorporating notions of creative thinking and thus choice, are in many ways more akin to the rational actor model. Each tradition nonetheless proposes that the personality is developed during the early formative childhood years of the individual through a process of learning.

Psychodynamic theories

Psychodynamic theories have their origins in the work of Sigmund Freud (1856–1939) and his ideas about how our personalities develop as an outcome of our intimate relationships with our parents, in particular, our mothers. His assertion that sexuality is present from birth and has a subsequent course of development is the fundamental basis of psychoanalysis.

In the psychoanalytical model, the human personality has three sets of interacting forces: 1) the id, or primitive biological drives; 2) the superego – or conscience – that operates in the unconsciousness but which is comprised of values internalised through the early interactions of the child, in particular those with their parents; and 3) the ego, or the conscious personality, which has the important task of balancing the demands of the id against the inhibitions imposed by the superego, as the child responds to external influences (Freud 1927).

Freud proposed two different explanations of offending behaviour. First, some forms of criminal activity are the product of mental disturbance or illness. His theory of psychosexual development proposes a number of complex stages of psychic development that may easily be disrupted, leading to neuroses or severe difficulties in adults. Crucially, a disturbance at one or more of these stages can lead to criminal behaviour in later life. Of central importance is the nature of the relationship the child has with its parents. Significantly, many influences are unconscious, with neither the child nor its parents aware of the impact they are having on each other.

Second, Freud argued that offenders possess a 'weak conscience', the development of which is of fundamental importance in the upbringing of the child. A sense of morality is closely linked to guilt, and those possessing the greatest degree of unconscious 'guilt' are likely to be those with the strictest consciences and the most unlikely to offend. Guilt results not from committing crimes but from a deeply embedded feeling that develops in childhood, the outcome of the way in which the parents respond to transgressions. It is a theory which has led to a proliferation of tests attempting to measure conscience or levels of guilt, in the belief that this will allow a prediction of later offending behaviour.

The Freudian approach is firmly embedded in the predestined actor model: unconscious conflicts or tensions determine all actions and it is the purpose of the conscious (ego) to resolve these tensions by finding ways to satisfy the basic inner urges by engaging in activities sanctioned by society such as playing organised sport or involvement in drama or artistic activities.

Later Freudians were concerned with elaborating the development of the ego more specifically. Aichhorn (1925) argued that at birth a child is unaware of the norms of society but has certain instinctive drives that demand satisfaction. The child is in an 'asocial state'. The task is to bring it into a social state but when the development process is ineffective he or she remains asocial. Thus, if the instinctive drives are not acted out, the child becomes suppressed and is in a state of 'latent delinquency'. Given outside provocative stimuli, this can be transformed into actual offending behaviour.

Healy and Bronner (1936) sought to explain why siblings exposed to similar unfavourable circumstances might react differently, with one becoming an offender and the others not. Offenders were found to be more emotionally disturbed, needing to express their frustrations through deviant activities, while non-offenders channelled their frustrated needs into socially accepted activities. Kate Friedlander (1947) argued that some children simply develop an antisocial behaviour or a faulty character that leaves them susceptible to deviant behaviour. Redl and Wineman (1951) argued that some children develop a delinquent ego and a subsequent hostile attitude towards authority because they have not developed a good ego and superego.

John Bowlby (1952) influentially argued that offending takes place when a child has not enjoyed a close and continuous relationship with its mother during its formative years. His maternal deprivation theory had a major and lasting influence on the training of social workers, while a plethora of researchers sought to test it empirically. Rutter (1981) conducted a comprehensive review of these studies and concluded that the stability of the child/mother relationship is more important than the absence of breaks and proposed that a small number of substitutes can successfully carry out mothering functions provided such care is good quality. The crucial issue is the quality of child-rearing practices.

Glueck and Glueck (1950) found that the fathers of offenders generally provide lax and inconsistent discipline, with the use of physical punishment common and the giving of praise rare. McCord, McCord and Zola (1959) agree that the consistency of discipline is more important than the degree of strictness, while Bandura and Walters (1959) found fathers of aggressive boys more likely to punish such behaviour in the home while approving of it outside.

Hoffman and Saltzstein (1967) identified three types of child-rearing techniques: 1) power assertion, involving the parental use of physical punishment and/or the withdrawal of material privileges; 2) love withdrawal, where the parent withdraws affection from the child, for example by paying no attention to it; 3) induction, entailing letting the child know how its actions have affected the parent, thus encouraging a sympathetic or empathetic response. The first technique primarily relies on the instillation of fear, while the other two depend on the fostering of guilt feelings in the child. The researchers concluded that children who have been nurtured through the use of love withdrawal or induction techniques develop greater internalised controls and are less likely to offend than those raised through power assertion techniques.

Research has suggested that a 'broken home', where one of the birth parents is not present, may be a factor in the development of offending.

Glueck and Glueck (1950) found that 60 per cent of the offenders in their sample came from such a home, a finding supported in Britain by Burt (1945) and Mannheim (1948). Others have observed that the 'broken home' is not a homogenous category and a range of different factors need to be considered (Tappan 1960). Nye (1958) and Gibbens (1963) found offending behaviour more likely to occur among children from intact but unhappy homes. West and Farrington (1973) found that about twice as many offenders as non-offenders came from homes broken by parental separation before the child was ten years old. Monahan (1957) suggested that broken homes were far more common among black than white offenders, while Chilton and Markle (1972) found that the rate of family breakdown was much higher in black than in white families and suggested that this may explain why more black young offenders come from broken homes. Pitts (1986) claimed a link between criminality and homelessness and found that black youths were more likely to become homeless than whites. Significantly, studies have found that broken homes and early separation predict convictions up to the age of 33 where the separation occurred before the age of five (Farrington 1992).

Behavioural learning theories

Behavioural theories have their origins in the work of Ivan Pavlov, who famously studied the processes involved in very simple, automatic animal behaviours, and BF Skinner who extended the behaviourist conditioning principle to active learning, where the animal has to do something in order to obtain a reward or avoid punishment. These theories propose that the behaviours we learn in our childhood are caused, strengthened or weakened by external stimuli in our environment and are an automatic response without thought or reflection.

Operant conditioning is thus a method of learning that occurs through rewards and punishments, which become associated with certain behaviours. Children might complete homework to earn a reward from a parent or teacher. In this example, the promise or possibility of a reward causes a qualitative increase in behaviour. But operant conditioning can also be used to reduce less desirable activities. For example, a child may be told they will have privileges withdrawn if they misbehave or talk in class and it is this potential for punishment that may lead to a decrease in disruptive behaviour.

Cognitive learning theories

Cognitive learning theories have their foundations in a fundamental critique of the predestined actor model and explain human behaviour in terms of a three-way dynamic reciprocity, in which personal factors, environmental influences and behaviour continually interact. Cognitivists share the view of the operant conditioning perspective that the individual must actively respond to stimuli if they are to learn but shift the emphasis to mental rather than physical activity. This social learning theory emphasises that behaviour may be reinforced not only through actual rewards and punishments but also through expectations that are learned by watching what happens to other people. Ultimately the person will make a choice as to what they will learn and how.

An early proponent of the notion that crime is simply a normal learned behaviour was Gabriel Tarde (1843–1904), who argued that offenders are primarily normal people who by accident of birth are brought up in a situation where in they learn crime as a way of life. His laws of imitation propose that people imitate and copy each other in proportion to the amount of contact they have. First, the law of close contact proposes that if a juvenile is regularly in the company of offenders they are more likely to imitate this behaviour than that of non-offenders with whom they have little association. Second, the law of imitation of superiors by inferiors proposes that youngsters imitate older individuals. Children hanging out on the street thus tend to take their cues and are heavily influenced by older children. Third, the law of insertion proposes that new activities and behaviours are superimposed on old ones and subsequently either reinforce or discourage previous customs. This law refers to the power said to be inherent in newness or novelty, where new fashions replace old 'customs'. Thus illicit drug taking may become popular among a group of juveniles who have previously favoured alcohol.

The work of Gabriel Tarde has been very influential. Social psychologists propose that patterns of illicit drug use may have their origins in the observation of parental drug use, which begins to have a damaging effect on children as young as two years old (Wills *et al* 1996). However, children respond to peer group influences more readily than adults because of the crucial role these relationships play in identity formation. Their greater desire for acceptance and approval from their peers makes them more susceptible to peer influences as they adjust their behaviour and attitudes to conform to those of their contemporaries. Significantly, young people 'commit crimes, as they live their lives, in groups' (Morse 1997a: 108). This important concept is explored further below. More indirectly, the desire of juveniles for peer approval can affect the choices they make without any direct coercion. Morse (1997b) observed that peers may provide models for behaviour that juveniles believe will assist them in accomplishing their own ends.

Edwin H Sutherland (1937) used the term differential association when influentially arguing that it is the frequency and consistency of contacts with patterns of criminality that determine the chances that a person will participate in systematic criminal behaviour. The basic cause of such behaviour is the existence of different cultural groups with different normative structures within the same society that have produced a situation of differential social organisation. He later argued that criminal behaviour occurs when individuals acquire sufficient sentiments in favour of criminality to outweigh their association with non-criminal tendencies (Sutherland 1947). The associations or contacts that have the greatest impact are those that are frequent, early in point of origin or the most intense.

Akers (1985) later restated the theory and focused on four central concepts. First, *differential association* refers to the patterns of interactions with others that are the source of social learning and which can be either favourable or unfavourable to offending. The indirect influence of more distant reference groups such as the media is now also recognised, including internet access, which can bring likeminded people together from all around the world (Hopkins Burke and Pollock 2004). Second, *definitions* reflect the meanings that a person applies to their own behaviour, for example the wider peer group might not define recreational drug use as deviant. Third, *differential reinforcement* refers to the actual or anticipated consequences of a particular behaviour: thus children will do things they think will result in rewards and avoid activities they think will result in punishment. Fourth, *imitation* involves observing what others do, but whether a decision is made to imitate that behaviour will depend on the characteristics of the person being observed, the actual behaviour the person engages in, and the observed consequences of that behaviour for others. If the observed young person appears to be 'cool', is engaged in activities that appear to be 'cool', rewarding and/or pleasurable, it is likely that the behaviour will be imitated.

Sociological theories

Sociological theories reject the individualist explanations favoured by the biological and psychological perspectives and examine the environmental factors that are considered to be the most important in the creation of crime and criminal behaviour. It is an enduring tradition, informed by the influential social theory of Emile Durkheim and his concerns with the social problems created by rapid social change.

Social disorganisation thesis

Durkheim (1933; originally 1893) provided two arguments to explain the rise in crime in modern industrial societies. First, such societies encourage a state of unbridled 'egoism' – the notion that individuals should pursue their own rational self-interest without reference to the collective interest of society – which is contrary to the maintenance of social solidarity and conformity to the law. Second, the likelihood of inefficient regulation is greater at a time of rapid modernisation because new forms of control have not evolved sufficiently to replace the older and now less appropriate means of maintaining solidarity. In such a period, society is in a state of normlessness or 'anomie', a condition characterised by a breakdown in norms and common understandings.

Durkheim claimed that without external controls human beings have unlimited aspirations; it is therefore appropriate for society to indicate the extent of acceptable rewards. This works reasonably well in times of social stability, but at times of economic upheaval, society is unable to control the ambitions of individuals. Thus, during an economic depression, people are forced to lower their sights, a situation which some will find intolerable, and yet when there is an improvement in economic conditions social equilibrium will break down, with uncontrollable desires released. Both situations can lead to increased criminality, the first through need and the second through greed. The social disorganisation thesis was later developed by sociologists based at the University of Chicago.

Ernest Burgess (1928) argued that as modern industrial cities expand in size their development is patterned socially. He observed that commercial enterprises were located in the central business district, with the most expensive residential areas in the outer suburbs, away from the bustle of the city centre and the homes of the poor. It was the 'zone in transition', what we might term the inner city in contemporary Britain, which contained rows of deteriorating tenements, often built in the shadow of ageing factories, that was the centre of attention. The outward expansion of the business district led to the constant displacement of residents and, as the least desirable living area, the zone was the focus for the influx of waves of immigrants who were too poor to reside elsewhere. Burgess observed that these social patterns weakened family and communal ties and resulted in social disorganisation and criminal behaviour.

Clifford Shaw and Henry McKay (1972; originally 1931) found that crime levels were highest in the slum neighbourhoods of the zone of transition regardless of which ethnic group resided there and, significantly, as these groups moved to other zones, their offending rates correspondingly decreased. It was this observation that led to the conclusion that it is the nature of the neighbourhood that regulates involvement in crime not the characteristics of particular individuals. The researchers emphasised the importance of neighbourhood organisation in allowing or preventing juvenile offending. In the more affluent communities, parents fulfilled the needs of their offspring and carefully supervised their activities; in the zone of transition, families and other conventional institutions were strained, if not destroyed, by rapid urban growth, migration and poverty. Left to their own devices, juveniles were not subject to the social constraints placed on those in more affluent areas and were more likely to seek excitement and friends on the street.

Shaw and McKay (1972: 174) concluded that disorganised neighbourhoods help produce and sustain 'criminal traditions' that compete with conventional values and can be 'transmitted down through successive generations of boys, in much the same way that language and other social forms are transmitted'. Thus, children growing up in socially disorganised inner city slum areas, characterised by the existence of a value system that condones criminal behaviour, could readily learn these values in their daily interactions with older adolescents. In short, the US variant of social disorganisation theory called for efforts to reorganise communities with treatment programmes that attempted to reverse the criminal learning of offenders. Juvenile offenders should be placed in settings where they received pro-social reinforcement, for example through the use of positive peer counselling and mentoring.

Durkheim proposed that human needs or aspirations were 'natural' in the sense that they socially constructed through reference to other individuals and groups. His US successor Robert Merton, by contrast, argued that needs were usually socially learned while – and this is the central component of his argument – there were social structural limitations imposed on access to the means to achieve these goals. Merton (1938) observed that it is possible to overemphasise either the goals or the means, with the outcome being social strains or 'anomie'. Deviant, especially criminal, behaviour results when cultural goals are accepted – and, for example, people would like to be materially successful – but where access to the means to achieve that goal is limited by the position of the individual in the social structure. In some cases, where the individual has limited access to the legitimate means of material success, they will adopt innovative strategies for attaining their objective, which include criminality.

Deviant subculture theories

Deviant subculture theories originated in the USA during the 1950s and, while there are different versions, all propose that some social groups have values and attitudes that encourage members to offend. Juveniles come together and engage in activities that may or may not be criminal because, in the language of today, they appear to be 'cool' and the individual can gain 'respect' from their peers.

Albert Cohen (1955) observed that offending was prevalent among lower-class males, with the most common form being the juvenile gang who were said to have values in opposition to those of the dominant culture. Delinquent boys came together to define status, with offending behaviour serving no real purpose and participants often discarding or destroying what they had stolen. They were simply a short-term hedonistic subculture: offending tends to be random and directed at people and property; stealing serves as a form of achieving peer status within the group. There is no other motive. It is simply cool.

Miller (1958) argued that working-class morality emerged as a response to living in the brutalised conditions of the slums, which encourages offending. His concept of focal concerns describes important aspects of participation in this working-class subculture. First, there is a concern over *trouble*: both getting into trouble and staying out of it are important daily preoccupations. Second, *toughness* represents commitment to breaking the law and being a problem to others, with machismo and daring emphasised. Third, *smartness* is the ability to gain some advantage by outsmarting or conning others. Fourth, *excitement* is living on the edge and doing dangerous things for 'the buzz' and which are 'cool'. Fifth, *fate* is of crucial concern, with many believing their lives to be subject to forces outside their control. Sixth, *autonomy* signifies being independent, not relying on others and a rejection of authority.

Cloward and Ohlin (1960) combined strain, differential association and social disorganisation perspectives in their differential opportunity theory. They argued that delinquent subcultures flourish among the lower classes but take different forms, with the means to achieve illegitimate success no more equally distributed than for legitimate success. They proposed three different variants of subculture and argued that the capacity for each to flourish is dependent on the locality in which they develop and the availability of deviant opportunities. First, *criminal* gangs emerge in localities where conventional as well as non-conventional values are integrated through the close connection of illegitimate and legitimate businesses.

Older criminals serve as role models, teach the necessary criminal skills and provide available opportunities and a career structure. Second, the *conflict or violent* gang is a non-stable and non-integrated grouping, which exists where there is an absence of a stable criminal organisation, and its members seek a reputation and respect for toughness and destructive violence. Third, the *retreatist* gang is equally unsuccessful in the pursuit of illegitimate or legitimate opportunities and members are seen to be double failures, retreating into a world of sex, drugs and alcohol.

Spergel (1964) identified an 'anomie gap' between aspirations, expected occupations and income, finding that the extent of this differed significantly between offenders, non-offenders and different subcultures. He introduced his own three-part subculture typology. First, a *racket* subculture develops in areas where organised adult criminality is already in existence and highly visible; second, a *theft* subculture, involving offences such as burglary, shoplifting, taking and driving away cars, develops where a criminal subculture already exists but is not very well established; and third, *conflict* subcultures involve gang fighting and the pursuit of reputation where there is limited or no access to either criminal or conventional activities. Drug misuse was found to be common to all subcultures as part of the transition from juvenile delinquent activity to conventional or fully developed criminal activity.

These early US deviant subcultural theories were widely accused of being overly determinist, with offenders seen to be not only different from non-offenders but in some way committed to an alternative 'ethical' code which made criminal involvement virtually compulsory and from which they could not escape. Now, while it is likely that some young people are so strongly socialised into the mores of a particular worldview through membership of a particular ethnic group, their upbringing and/or the reinforcing influences of neighbourhood groups or gangs that they do not challenge this heritage in any way, it is likely that many others have less consistent socialisation experiences and a far more tangential relationship to deviant behaviour.

The most comprehensive critique of the overly determinist, early deviant subcultural tradition is given by Sykes and Matza (1957), who crucially observed that these studies failed to explain why it is that most young offenders 'grow out' of their criminality. Their drift theory proposes that juveniles sense a moral obligation to be bound to the law and if that bond remains in place they will remain law abiding most of the time. It is when that bond is not in place that the juvenile will drift between involvement in legitimate and illegitimate activities. Most juvenile offenders actually hold values, beliefs and attitudes very similar to those of law-abiding citizens. This being the case, the issue is how they can justify their involvement in criminality to themselves. The answer is that they learn 'techniques' which enable them to 'neutralise' their law-abiding values and attitudes temporarily and thus drift back and forth between legitimate and illegitimate behaviours. Much of the time such juveniles participate in conventional activities but shun these while offending. In such situations, the individual disregards the controlling influences of rules and values and utilises techniques of neutralisation to weaken the hold society has over them. In other words, these techniques act as defence mechanisms that release the young person from the constraints associated with the moral order.

Matza (1964) rejected the notion that juveniles maintain a set of values that are independent of the dominant culture, proposing that they appreciate the culturally held goals and expectations of the middle class but feel the pursuit of such aspirations would be frowned on by their peers as they are not 'cool'. Moreover, such beliefs remain almost unconscious – or subterranean – because young people fear expressing them to their peers. It is when they reach a situation where they can admit these feelings to a close friend that they will simply grow out of offending. Of course, some never do and it is these juveniles who develop adult criminal careers.

Early British deviant subcultural studies followed the lead of the US theories. Mays (1954) argued that, in some working-class areas, the residents share a number of attitudes and ways of behaving that predispose them to criminality. Working-class culture is not intentionally criminal; it is just a different socialisation, which, at times, happens to be contrary to the law. Criminal behaviour is not a conscious rebellion against middle-class values but is part of an alternative subculture that has developed over the years in a random sort of way. Morris (1957) observed that the family controls middle-class socialisation, is very ordered and almost all activities are centred on the home and the family. By contrast, the socialisation of the working-class child tends to be divided between family, peer group and street acquaintances, with the latter likely to have a less ordered and regulated upbringing. The peer group is a much stronger influence from a much earlier age among the working classes, who encounter controls only after they have transgressed and are processed by the criminal justice system. The whole ethos of the working class is oriented towards antisocial and criminal behaviour.

Downes (1966) found that a large amount of offending happened in street corner groups rather than organised gangs. Status frustration did not occur to a significant degree but the typical response to a lack of success at school or work was one of dissociation. There was an emphasis on leisure activities, with a dominant interest in commercial forms of entertainment, rather than youth clubs with their middle-class orientation, but access was nevertheless restricted by lack of money and juveniles would take part in petty criminality to find excitement. Peter Wilmott (1966) also found that offending was simply part of a general lower working-class subculture. Teenagers became involved in petty crime simply for the fun and togetherness of a shared activity.

Parker (1974) conducted a survey of unskilled adolescents in an area of Liverpool with a high rate of youth offending and found a pattern of loosely knit peer groups with criminality a central activity. Young males shared common problems such as unemployment, while leisure opportunities were limited and consequently some of their number developed a solution in the form of stealing car radios. The community in which they lived largely condoned this behaviour as long as the victims were from outside the area.

These British subcultural studies are important because they identify specific historical factors, in particular the level of economic activity and the importance of a structural class analysis in helping to explain youth offending (Hopkins Burke and Sunley 1998). The concept was subsequently revised and revitalised by radical sociologists based at the Birmingham Centre for Contemporary Cultural Studies in the 1970s who pertinently observed that youth subcultures arise at particular historical 'moments' as cultural solutions to the same structural economic problems created by rapid social change. The focus was on two broad areas: 1) mainstream youth and delinquency and 2) expressive or spectacular youth subcultures.

Two major studies of mainstream youth subcultures are those of Willis (1977) and Corrigan (1979), both concerned with the transition from school to work among urban lower working-class boys. Their 'problem' was found to be an alien or irrelevant education system followed by the prospect of a boring and dead-end job, and the 'solution' was a 'culture of resistance' manifested in truancy and petty offending, albeit during a period of relative full employment. 'Spectacular' youth subcultures – such as teddy boys, mods, skinheads and punks – involved the adoption, by young people of both sexes, of an idiosyncratic style of dress combined with distinctive lifestyles, behaviour patterns and musical preferences. The Birmingham studies represent an important development of the subcultural tradition because they recognise that particular subcultures have arisen in response to economic problems encountered by different groups of young people at particular historical moments.

Hopkins Burke and Sunley (1998) observe that these studies presume a linear development of history where different subcultures arise, coalesce, fade and are replaced as economic circumstances change: for example, the mods were a product of the upwardly mobile working classes during the optimistic 1960s whereas the punks were a product of the 'dole queue' despondency of the late 1970s. The researchers note the subsequent co-existence of different subcultures and observe that these are the product of a fragmented society where different groups of young people have coalesced to create solutions to their specific socio-economic problems. Central to this account is the possibility of choice. The simultaneous existence of different subcultures enables some young people to choose the solution to their problem from the various subcultures available, although that choice will be crucially and significantly constrained by structural factors, not least those of (often multiple) social exclusion.

Earlier subcultural studies suggest that young people have limited choices, if any, between the deviant subculture available at a particular time and its location and a life of conventionality. A more contemporary interpretation of youth subcultures enables us to recognise that individuals, and different groups of young people, have had very different experiences of the radical economic change that has occurred in Britain since the late 1970s.

Social control theories

Criminological theories usually view conformity to be the natural state of humanity and that criminal behaviour is simply abnormal. Social control theories challenge this orthodox way of thinking about crime. Thus the central question asked is not the usual why do some people commit crime? Rather, it is why do most of us conform? The unifying factor in the different versions of control theory is that criminality is to be expected when social and personal controls fail to restrain the individual from criminal involvement.

Early control theories attached more importance to psychological factors. Reiss (1951) distinguished between the effects of personal control, where individuals internalise the norms and rules of non-deviant primary groups to the extent that they become their own, and social controls, where external social groups or institutions make rules or norms effective. Reiss considered personal controls to be far more important in preventing deviance than external social controls.

Nye (1958) identified four modes of social control that encourage conformity in juveniles. First, *direct* control is imposed through external forces such as parents, teachers and the police, using direct restraint and punishment. Second, individuals themselves, in the absence of external regulation, exercise *internalised* control. Third, *indirect* control is dependent on the degree of affection an individual has for conventional significant others. Fourth, control through *alternative means* of needs satisfaction works by reducing the temptation for individuals to resort to illegitimate means. Though independent of each other, these four modes of control are mutually reinforcing and work effectively together.

Reckless (1967) sought to explain why, despite the various push and pull factors that may tempt individuals to break the law, most people remain law abiding. He argued that a combination of control factors, both internal and external to the individual, serve as insulators or 'containments' but attached much more importance to internal factors, arguing that these tend to control the individual irrespective of external environment change. First, individuals with a strong and favourable *self-concept* are better insulated against factors that encourage criminal involvement. Second, *goal orientation* is the extent to which the person has a clear direction in life, oriented towards the achievement of legitimate goals such as education and career. Third, *frustration tolerance* is where contemporary society with its emphasis on individualism and immediate gratification might generate considerable frustration. Fourth, *norm retention* is the extent to which individuals accept, internalise and are committed to conventional laws, norms, values and rules and the institutions that represent and uphold these.

Travis Hirschi (1969) has made the most influential contribution to social control theory and notes that, at their simplest level, all such theories share the basic assumption that offending behaviour occurs when the individual bond to legitimate society is weak or broken. He identified four elements of the social bond. First, *attachment* refers to the capacity of individuals to form effective relationships with other people and institutions: in the case of children, with their parents, peers and school. Second, *commitment* refers to the social investments made by the individual to conventional activities that could be put at risk by engaging in criminal behaviour. Third, *involvement* refers to the simple reality that a person may be too busy doing conventional things to find time to engage in deviant activities. Fourth, *beliefs* are a set of impressions and convictions needing constant reinforcement, closely connected to the pattern and strength of attachments an individual has to other people and institutions. These variables, though independent, are highly interrelated and help to prevent law-breaking activities in most people.

Subsequent research has found that the aspects of the social bond most consistently related to offending behaviour are those of the family and the school and there is substantial evidence that juveniles with strong attachments to their family are less likely to offend. The evidence on the association between attachment and commitment to school, particularly poor school performance, not liking school and low educational and occupational aspirations and delinquency, is even stronger (Hopkins Burke 2008).

Researchers have subsequently sought to strengthen control theory by integrating it with other theoretical perspectives. Elliot, Ageton and Canter (1979) expanded and synthesised anomie theories, social learning and social control perspectives, their starting point being that individuals have different early socialisation experiences that lead to variable degrees of commitment to the conventional social order. These initial social bonds can be reinforced by positive experiences at school and in the wider community. The structural dimension is explicit in their analysis of the factors that serve to loosen social bonds, such as limited or blocked opportunities, including economic recession and unemployment.

Stephen Box (1981) combined control theory with a labelling/conflict perspective, arguing that differential policing practices and institutional biases at different stages of the criminal justice system operate very much to the detriment of the disadvantaged. Stigma and a sense of injustice can be provoked by the criminalisation process, which provides further impetus towards criminal behaviour. Box (1987) later showed how the impact of economic recession can fuel an increase in criminal activity. First, by further reducing legitimate opportunities and increasing deprivation, it produces more 'strain' and more individuals with a motive to deviate. The commitment of the person to society is undermined because their access to conventional modes of activity has been reduced. Second, by undermining the family and conventional employment prospects, the ability and motivation of an individual to develop an attachment to other human beings, who might introduce a controlling influence in their life, is substantially reduced.

John Braithwaite's (1989) theory of predatory crime integrates elements of control, labelling, strain and subcultural theory and proposes that the way to reduce crime is to have a commitment to reintegrative forms of shaming. A crucial distinction is made between the negative shaming characteristic of contemporary criminal justice systems, which leads to the stigmatising and outcasting of the individual, and shaming which is *reintegrative* and seeks to restore the individual to society. The orthodox approach merely pushes offenders toward criminal subcultures, which become increasingly attractive to the stigmatised individual seeking emotional and social support. Participation in these groups can also supply criminal role models, knowledge on how to offend and techniques of neutralisation, which, taken together, can make the choice to engage in crime more rational.

Gottfredson and Hirschi (1990) combined rational actor model notions of crime with a predestined actor model theory of criminality in order to produce a general theory of crime causation. Crime is defined as acts of force or fraud undertaken in pursuit of self-interest. It is argued that the vast bulk of criminal acts are trivial and mundane affairs that result in little gain and require little in the way of effort, planning, preparation or skill. Their 'versatility construct' considers crime to be essentially interchangeable: the characteristics of ordinary criminal events are simply inconsistent with notions of specialisation or the criminal career. The likelihood of criminal behaviour is closely linked to the availability of opportunity, the characteristics of situations and the personal properties of individuals and their level of self-control. This latter concept is not confined to criminal acts but also implicated in many analogous acts, such as promiscuity, alcohol use and smoking, where such behaviour is portrayed as the impulsive actions of disorganised individuals seeking quick gratification.

Gottfredson and Hirschi turn to the predestined actor model to account for variations in self-control and argue that the main cause is ineffective parenting, which is identified as a failing that cannot easily be remedied in later life. According to this 'stability postulate', levels of self-control will remain stable throughout the life course. By asserting that crime is essentially interchangeable, while the propensity to become involved in criminality remains stable, the theory has no need to provide different explanations for different types of crime, nor for primary or persistent secondary deviation.

Hirschi (1995) argued that policies designed to deter (the rational actor model) or rehabilitate (the predestined actor model) will continue to have little success in reducing crime, influentially proposing that effective policies will be those that support and enhance socialisation in the family by improving the quality of child-rearing practices, with the focus on the form, size and stability of the family unit. Thus, there should always be two parents for every child, no more than three children in a family, with the relationship between parents and children strong and durable. Furthermore, it is not young teenage mothers who are a problem; it is having a mother without a father. Effective policies are those that focus not on preventing teenage pregnancies but on maintaining the involvement of the father in the life of the child. Hirschi proposed that these polices would strengthen family bonds, increase positive socialisation and create greater self-control in the child.

Predestined actor model: conclusions and policy implications

The predestined actor model proposes that juveniles become offenders because of individual or social factors in their lives that cause or *determine* them to behave in ways over which they have little or no control. The solution is to remove or restrict the influence of these factors, for example, genetic predisposition to aggression can be countered by the provision of sporting or artistic diversionary activities, altered biological state factors can be reduced or eradicated by challenging alcohol or drug use, psychological factors can be countered by behavioural programmes to unlearn previously damaging behaviour, and environmental/sociological factors can be addressed by removing the juvenile from negative social environments. Offenders are most likely to desist from offending when these biological, psychological or sociological factors are addressed.

Victimised actor model theories

The victimised actor model proposes that the offender is the product of an unjust and unequal society where the behaviour and activities of the poor and socially excluded are invariably targeted and criminalised by criminal justice agencies.

Table 3: Victimised actor model

▶ The offender is the victim of an unjust and unequal society

▶ The behaviour and activities of the poor and powerless sections of society are targeted and criminalised

▶ Neither punishment nor treatment of offenders is proposed but non-criminalisation and measures introduced to reduce unequal power relations and improve the life chances of the individual.

(Adapted from Hopkins Burke 2008: 150)

Labelling theories

The central proposition of labelling theories is that it is the reactions of other people, or an audience, that is the most important variable in the ongoing process of action. Thus Albert Cohen (1955) emphasised how the negative and malicious characteristics of young offender activities can encourage a strong societal reaction, which leads to them being categorised as abnormal and unacceptable. The outcome is the denial of legitimate opportunities for young people labelled as deviant and this encourages them to pursue illegitimate activities.

Cohen (1972) instigated an interest in the activities of prominent agents of social reaction, using the term 'moral panic'. His account of how the media amplified the initially rather innocuous mods and rocker 'riots' that occurred at Clacton during Easter 1964 is now well known to criminology students. The media stereotyped and polarised the contending groups (not only mods and rockers but juveniles in general and the police) and increased the sensitivity of the participants, which encouraged further delinquent behaviour.

Social reactions have also been studied at the micro-level and this brings us to the classic work of Howard Becker (1963), who argued that, since social groups create rules, they also create deviants or outsiders. Deviancy is not about the quality of the act itself but about the social process of recognition and rule enforcement, and our attention is directed to the rule-makers and enforcers – the 'moral entrepreneurs' – as much as to deviants. Morality is an enterprise, not just a simple natural social process, and our attention is directed to the values of those who have the power to label (Becker 1967).

The work of Becker is the usual source of radical variants of labelling theory. His work implies there is no need to explain deviance in the first place, that it is simply a very common social activity, a normal one, which only becomes abnormal when it is so labelled by an outside audience. The application of the label confirms the initial diagnosis and becomes a self-fulfilling prophecy, launching juveniles on a deviant career from which they will have increasing difficulty leaving.

Conflict and radical theories

Conflict and radical theories developed the labelling and social reaction thesis further and sought to explain criminality in terms of the unequal nature of society. The former take a pluralist stance and observe that society consists of different groups with very different levels of economic power, all involved in a competitive struggle to promote their material interests, while the radical variants identify the power of the state to criminalise, make laws and prosecute offenders (Taylor, Walton and Young 1973).

There are two current variants of the radical tradition but only critical criminology has unequivocal foundations in the victimised actor model. These criminologists define criminality in terms of the concept of oppression and observe that some groups in society – the working class, women and minority ethnic groups – are the most likely to suffer oppressive social relations based on class division, sexism and racism. Criminal behaviour among such groups is seen to be the rational outcome of the interaction between the marginalisation or exclusion from access to mainstream institutions and that of criminalisation by the state authorities. The latter involves a process in which the law, agencies of social control and the media associate crime with particular groups who are subsequently identified and targeted as a threat (Scraton and Chadwick 1996; originally 1992).

Left realism is the other contemporary criminological perspective. It has its roots in the radical tradition but one that recognises that crime is a real problem for ordinary people, which must be taken seriously. Central to this perspective is the proposition that crime requires a comprehensive solution that is both 'tough on crime' but also 'tough on the causes of crime'. The first part of this equation proposes that offenders should accept and take responsibility for their actions and has its theoretical foundations in the rational actor model. The second part proposes a tough stance on the causes of crime by targeting the individual and in particular structural factors, such as poor education, lack of training and skills, poverty and lack of legitimate opportunities, which encourage criminality. It is therefore in accordance not only with the predestined actor model but also the victimised actor model. It is this dual emphasis on the juvenile offender taking responsibility for their actions, while at the same time tackling the often multiple factors of social exclusion, that has underpinned the work of youth offending teams (YOTs) since the establishment of the contemporary youth justice system (Hopkins Burke 2008).

Victimised actor model: conclusions and policy implications

The victimised actor model proposes that juvenile offenders are the product of a highly competitive but unequal society. Statistically, they are significantly over-represented among the ranks of the socially excluded, with invariably very limited life chances. The clear policy implication of this model is to significantly improve access to education, training and skills and thus enhance legitimate career opportunities. Offenders are likely to desist from criminal involvement when these exclusion needs are met and the juvenile has available legitimate opportunities.

Summary and conclusions

This chapter has considered how different criminological theories have at different times explained the offending behaviour of juveniles and by implication why it is that some offenders come to desist from criminal involvement. Three different models of offending behaviour have been identified and discussed: the rational actor model, which proposes that juvenile choices to offend are rational in the context of their lives and they should consequently take responsibility and accept appropriate punishment for their actions; the predestined actor model, which proposes that involvement in criminality is the outcome of factors, either internal or external to the individual, that lead them to behave in ways over which they have little or no control and which thus mitigate the extent of their culpability, with treatment being the preferred intervention; and the victimised actor model, which asserts that offenders are themselves the victims of an unequal and unjust society where the choices they make are invariably significantly restricted by the socially excluded circumstances in which they live their lives. It is clear that all three models can be legitimately utilised in order to address different components of the offending behaviour of the juvenile and explain the current orthodoxy in contemporary youth justice work (Hopkins Burke 2008).

References

Aichhorn A (1925) *Wayward Youth*. New York: Meridian Books.

Akers RL (1985) *Deviant Behaviour: A Social Learning Approach* (3rd edn). Belmont, CA: Wadsworth.

Baldwin JD (1990) 'The role of sensory stimulation in criminal behaviour, with special attention to the age peak in crime', in L Ellis and H Hoffman (eds) *Crime: Biological, Social and Moral Contexts*. New York: Praeger.

Bandura A and Walters RH (1959) *Adolescent Aggression*. New York: Ronald Press.

Becker GS (1968) 'Crime and punishment: an economic approach', *Journal of Political Economy*, 76(2): 169–217.

Becker H (1963) *Outsiders: Studies in the Sociology of Deviance*. New York: Free Press.

Becker H (1967) 'Whose side are we on?', *Social Problems*, 14(3): 239–247.

Bennett T (2000) *Drugs and Crime: The Results of the Second Developmental Stage of the New-Adam Programme*, Home Office research study 2005. London: Home Office.

Bowlby J (1952) *Maternal Care and Mental Health* (2nd edn). Geneva: World Health Organisation.

Box S (1981) *Deviance, Reality and Society* (2nd edn). London: Rinehart and Winston.

Box S (1987) *Recession, Crime and Punishment*. London: Macmillan.

Braithwaite J (1989) *Crime, Shame and Reintegration*. Cambridge: Cambridge University Press.

Burgess EW (1928) 'The growth of the city', in R Park, EW Burgess and RD McKenzie (eds) *The City*. Chicago, IL: University of Chicago Press.

Burt C (1945) *The Young Delinquent*. London: University of London Press.

Chilton RJ and Markle GE (1972) 'Family disruption, delinquent conduct, and the effect of subclassification', *American Sociological Review*, 37: 93–108.

Clarke RVG (1987) 'Rational choice theory and prison psychology', in BJ McGurk, D Thorton and M Williams (eds) *Applying Psychology to Imprisonment: Theory and Practice*. London: HMSO.

Cloward RA and Ohlin LE (1960) *Delinquency and Opportunity: A Theory of Delinquent Gangs*. New York: Free Press.

Cohen AK (1955) *Delinquent Boys: The Culture of the Gang*. New York: Free Press.

Cohen P (1972) 'Sub-cultural conflict and working class community', *Working Papers in Cultural Studies, No 2*. Birmingham: CCCS, University of Birmingham.

Cohen LE and Felson M (1979) 'Social inequality and predatory criminal victimization: an exposition and test of a formal theory', *American Sociological Review*, 44: 588–608.

Corrigan P (1979) *The Smash Street Kids*. London: Paladin.

Department of Health (2005) *Smoking, Drinking and Drug Use among Young People in England in 2004*. London: Department of Health.

Downes D (1966) *The Delinquent Solution*. London: Routledge & Kegan Paul.

Durkheim E (1933; originally 1893) *The Division of Labour in Society*. Glencoe, IL: Free Press.

Elliot D, Ageton S and Canter J (1979) 'An integrated theoretical perspective on delinquent behaviour', *Journal of Research in Crime and Delinquency*, 16: 126–149.

Ellis L and Crontz PD (1990) 'Androgens, brain functioning, and criminality: the neurohormonal foundations of antisociality', in L Ellis and H Hoffman (eds) *Crime in Biological, Social, and Moral Contexts*. New York: Praeger.

Farrington DP (1992) 'Juvenile delinquency', in JC Coleman (ed) *The School Years* (2nd edn). London: Routledge.

Felson M (1998) *Crime and Everyday Life* (2nd edn). Thousand Oaks, CA: Pine Forge.

Ferri E (1895) *Criminal Sociology*. London: Unwin.

Freud S (1927) *The Ego and the Id*. London: Hogarth.

Friedlander K (1947) *The Psychoanalytic Approach to Juvenile Delinquency*. London: Kegan Paul.

Gibbens TCN (1963) *Psychiatric Studies of Borstal Lads*. Oxford: Oxford University Press.

Glueck S and Glueck E (1950) *Unravelling Juvenile Delinquency*. Oxford: Oxford University Press.

Gottfredson MR and Hirschi T (1990) *A General Theory of Crime*. Stanford, CA: Stanford University Press.

Healy W and Bronner AF (1936) *New Light on Delinquency and its Treatment*. New Haven, CT: Yale University Press.

Hirschi T (1969) *Causes of Delinquency*. Berkeley, CA: University of California Press.

Hirschi T (1995) 'The family', in JQ Wilson and J Petersilia (eds) *Crime*. San Francisco, CA: ICS Press.

Hoffman ML and Saltzstein HD, (1967) 'Parent discipline and the child's moral development', *Journal of Personality and Social Psychology*, 5: 45.

Hopkins Burke RD (2008) *Young People, Crime and Justice*. Cullompton: Willan Publishing.

Hopkins Burke RD (2009) *An Introduction to Criminological Theory* (3rd edn). Cullompton: Willan Publishing.

Hopkins Burke RD and Pollock E (2004) 'A tale of two anomies: some observations on the contribution of (sociological) criminological theory to explaining hate crime motivation', *Internet Journal of Criminology*.

Hopkins Burke RD and Sunley R (1998) 'Youth subcultures in contemporary Britain', in K Hazelhurst and C Hazlehurst (eds) *Gangs and Youth Subcultures: International Explorations*. New Brunswick, NJ: Transaction Press.

Institute of Alcohol Studies (2005) *Adolescents and Alcohol*. St Ives, Cambridgeshire: IAS.

Jefferis BJMH, Power C and Manor O (2005) 'Adolescent drinking level and adult binge drinking in a national cohort', *Addiction*, 100(4): 543–549.

Jeffery CR (1977) *Crime Prevention through Environmental Design*. Beverly Hills, CA: Sage.

Jones S (1993) *The Language of the Genes*. London: Harper Collins.

Lombroso C (1875) *L'uomo delinquente (The Criminal Man)*. Milan: Hoepli.

McCord W, McCord J and Zola IK (1959) *Origins of Crime: A New Evaluation of the Cambridge-Somerville Youth Study*. New York: Columbia University Press.

Mannheim H (1948) *Juvenile Delinquency in an English Middletown*. London: Kegan Paul, Turner, Trubner and Co Ltd.

Matza DM (1964) *Delinquency and Drift*. New York: Wiley.

Mays JB (1954) *Growing Up in the City: A Study of Juvenile Delinquency in an Urban Neighbourhood*. Liverpool: Liverpool University Press.

Mednick SA, Moffit TE and Stack S (eds) (1987) *The Causes of Crime: New Biological Approaches*. Cambridge: Cambridge University Press.

Merton RK (1938) 'Social structure and anomie', *American Sociological Review*, 3: 672–682.

Miller WB (1958) 'Lower class culture as a generalising milieu of gang delinquency', *Journal of Social Issues*, 14: 5–19.

Monahan TP (1957) 'Family status and the delinquent child: a reappraisal and some new findings', *New Forces*, 35: 250–266.

Morris TP (1957) *The Criminal Area: A Study in Social Ecology*. London: Routledge & Kegan Paul.

Morse SM (1997a) 'Immaturity and irresponsibility', *Journal of Criminal Law and Criminology*, 88.

Morse SM (1997b) 'Delinquency and desert', *The ANNALS of the American Academy of Political and Social Science*, 564(1): 56–80.

Nye FI (1958) *Family Relationships and Delinquent Behaviour*. New York: Wiley.

Olwens D (1987) 'Testosterone and adrenaline: aggressive and antisocial behaviour in normal adolescent males', in SA Mednick, TE Moffit and S Stack (eds) *The Causes of Crime: New Biological Approaches*. Cambridge: Cambridge University Press.

Parker H (1974) *View from the Boys*. Newton Abbot: David and Charles.

Pitts J (1986) 'Black young people and juvenile crime: some unanswered questions', in R Matthews and J Young (eds) *Confronting Crime*. London: Sage.

Reckless W (1967) *The Crime Problem* (4th edn). New York: Appleton Century Crofts.

Redl F and Wineman D (1951) *Children Who Hate*. New York: Free Press.

Reiss AJ (1951) 'Delinquency as the failure of personal and social controls', *American Sociological Review*, 16: 213–239.

Rutter M (1981) *Maternal Deprivation Reassessed*. Harmondsworth: Penguin.

Schalling D (1987) 'Personality correlates of plasma testosterone levels in young delinquents: an example of person–situation interaction', in SA Mednick, TE Moffit and SA Stack (eds) *The Causes of Crime: New Biological Approaches*. Cambridge: Cambridge University Press.

Scraton P and Chadwick K (1996; originally 1992) 'The theoretical priorities of critical criminology', in J Muncie, E McLaughlin and M Langan (eds) *Criminological Perspectives: A Reader*. London: Sage.

Shaw CR and McKay HD (1972; originally 1931) *Juvenile Delinquency and Urban Areas*. Chicago, IL: University of Chicago Press.

Sheldon WH (1949) *Varieties of Delinquent Youth*. London: Harper.

Shoenthaler SJ (1982) 'The effects of blood sugar on the treatment and control of antisocial behaviour: a double-blind study of an incarcerated juvenile population', *International Journal for Biosocial Research*, 3: 1–15.

Spergel IA (1964) *Racketsville, Slumtown, Haulburg*. Chicago, IL: University of Chicago Press.

Sykes G and Matza D (1957) 'Techniques of neutralization: a theory of delinquency', *American Sociological Review*, 22: 664–670.

Sutherland EH (1937) *The Professional Thief: By a Professional Thief*. Chicago, IL: University of Chicago Press.

Sutherland EH (1947) *Principles of Criminology* (4th edn). Philadelphia, PA: Lippincott.

Tappan PW (1960) *Crime, Justice and Correction*. New York: McGraw-Hill.

Taylor I, Walton P and Young J (1973) *The New Criminology: For a Social Theory of Deviance*. London: Routledge & Kegan Paul.

Virkkunen M (1987) 'Metabolic dysfunctions amongst habitually violent offenders: reactive hypoglycaemia and cholesterol levels', in SA Mednick, TE Moffit and SA Stack (eds) *The Causes of Crime: New Biological Approaches*. Cambridge: Cambridge University Press.

West DJ and Farrington DP (1973) *Who Becomes Delinquent?* London: Heinemann.

Willis P (1977) *Learning to Labour*. London: Saxon House.

Wills TA, Vaccaro D, McNamara G and Hirky EA (1996) 'Escalated substance use: a longitudinal grouping analysis from early to middle adolescence', *Journal of Abnormal Psychology*, April: 166-180.

Wilmott P (1966) *Adolescent Boys in East London*. London: Routledge & Kegan Paul.

Wilson JQ and Herrnstein RJ (1985) *Crime and Human Nature*. New York: Simon and Schuster.

Wright RA (1993) 'A socially sensitive criminal justice system', in JW Murphy and DL Peck (eds) *Open Institutions: The Hope for Democracy*. Westport, CT: Praeger.

2
Troubled or troublesome. Safeguarding children in the youth justice system: custody and community

Maggie Blyth

Children in all age groups can be vulnerable so it is important that ... services also address the needs of older children to provide a timely offer of help to teenagers. The importance of early help for this age group is as vital as it is for young children.

(Munro 2011: 9)

Understanding what works in child protection and the practice that should be implemented by all agencies working with young people is fundamental to youth justice services. Furthermore, the effective protection of children and young people involves sound judgement of risk at a practice and organisational level, and this is of particular importance to those working in youth offending teams (YOTs) or with young people incarcerated in the secure estate. Indeed, services for predominantly very vulnerable children and young people can present challenges to all frontline staff, particularly at a time when the reorganisation of public services is impacting on the configuration of resources at the 'front door'.

In May 2011, Professor Eileen Munro published her final report on the review of the child protection system in this country. *A Child-centred System* (Munro 2011) makes a number of recommendations for government and the multi-agency child protection system. She reported on progress against her recommendations in June 2012 (Munro 2012), making the general observation that if her proposed reforms were to have sufficient impact they would need to be fully implemented in the light of all the other changes currently taking place across the public sector.

The Munro review is central to the safeguarding of children and young people and it is important that practitioners working in YOTs and other youth justice settings are familiar with the assumptions that underpin the recommendations. Safeguarding children and young people has significant implications for multi-agency working – that is, all statutory agencies tasked with child protection duties, including voluntary and community organisations that may be in place to provide early support.

Introduction

This chapter explores the challenges practitioners face in relation to safeguarding children and young people in the youth justice system. It discusses some of the themes emerging from the government's response to the Munro review and analyses the extent to which the Munro recommendations fit the youth justice system.

Current policy relating to national child protection arrangements is considered first, with particular emphasis on the impact of the new 'localism' agenda and the Department for Education's *Working Together* documentation, including the revised guidance out for consultation as this report goes to press (HM Government 2012). The chapter goes on to examine the child's journey through the child protection system – from early contact and referral to children's specialist services through to assessment, intervention and receiving help. Attention is given to those groups of vulnerable older adolescents, young carers and children who suffer hidden harm as a result of parental mental health, substance misuse, domestic abuse or sexual exploitation. The increasing evidence that some older adolescents fail to attract supportive interventions and, coupled with a drift into the youth justice system, increase their risk of going missing, becoming homeless or transparent to the wider child protection arrangements is also explored. The first half of the contribution concludes that there must be clear lines of accountability for child protection at a national and local level to ensure that services for the most vulnerable young people remain in place and considers the extent to which local safeguarding children boards (LSCBs) can provide the necessary scrutiny and oversight of child protection arrangements across a local area and champion the needs of older young people.

Second, the chapter examines opportunities for reviewing multi-agency working, ensuring closer integration between children's services and youth justice and that links are not lost between adult and children's services as a whole. It argues that safeguarding is the flipside of public protection and that real difficulties remain when young people's needs are overlooked in assessments of adult capability or matters related to domestic abuse, parental mental illness and adolescent on parent violence. It also explores the lessons learned from serious case reviews (SCRs) over recent years and concludes that, as services move to a system promoting greater professional judgement, it is vital that local multi-agency systems improve monitoring, learning and adapting their practice. The proposed alignment of the Youth Justice Board (YJB) serious incident reporting framework with SCRs at local level is broadly welcomed. The YJB has set out its plans for protection of the public from youth crime and for safeguarding the most vulnerable young people (YJB 2012).

Third, early intervention and prevention services in the context of safeguarding are discussed. Munro defined the term 'early help', and this is examined in relation to the success of prevention services over the past decade. The chapter emphasises the need to use evidence-based practice in determining policy and asks how YOTs can maintain the prevention element of their work amid public sector reorganisation. The numbers of children entering the child protection system rose dramatically in the three years following the public outcry of 2008 in response to the death of Peter Connolly, and although steadying in many parts of the country, there remains uncertainty about the strength of prevention services at local level. It is questionable whether local partnerships can adequately configure services so that prevention strategies properly impact on, and indeed reduce, the numbers of children and young people referred to acute services as a result of maltreatment or perceived high levels of complex need (CIB 2012). The economic austerity shows no sign of relenting over the foreseeable future and the numbers of vulnerable children are already on the rise, with 200,000 more living in poverty than in 2004 (Brewer, Browne and Joyce 2011). The ability of agencies to deliver early help as the impact of financial pressures on the public sector continues must be appraised.

Whose business is safeguarding?

In England, the official description of safeguarding is located in the statutory guidance outlined in *Working Together* (HM Government 2010) and its current suggested revisions (HM Government 2012). The concept of serious harm is used as a basis for deciding what state intervention should take place when a child or young person is considered at risk.

The *Every Child Matters* reforms of the early part of the 21st century were intended to embed child protection into the work of all professionals who have a role in keeping children safe. At their heart was partnership working, particularly between social services, police, education and health (HM Government 2004). The Children Act 2004 placed a duty of co-operation on local agencies and local authorities to work together. *Working Together*, in 2010 and 2012, is explicit about this expectation. Against this landscape, the reforms to the public sector have implications for how the *Working Together* guidance will be implemented in a meaningful manner at local level.

Recent school reforms focus primarily on educational attainment and there is no longer significant reference to the importance of schools contributing to a child's overall health and wellbeing. It was only when the Lords intervened in late 2011 that the proposed removal of the duty on schools to co-operate with local authorities was overturned and, despite this amendment, the framework for schools remains very narrow, concentrating on raising standards and curriculum reform rather than addressing schools' responsibilities in protecting children from maltreatment. Similarly, the health reforms are in danger of entirely overlooking the needs of young people. The establishment of several hundred clinical commissioning groups (CCGs) from autumn 2012 will place GP consortia at the head of commissioning services for the most vulnerable children and young people. It is still not clear how safeguarding arrangements will be integrated into the new arrangements. With waiting lists for child and adolescent mental health services still unacceptably high in some areas of the country, and with changes to the way that designated professionals work, this may hinder some of the work of the past decade in identifying harm and abuse among adolescents. Towards the end of 2012/13 new police and crime commissioners will hold responsibility for the configuration of local policing budgets and this will undoubtedly impact on youth justice services at a local level and on public protection units, at worst resulting in reduced availability for partnership work in the area of safeguarding. YOTs are encouraged to work with local partners to provide evidence for particular needs of children and young people at risk in their areas (YJB/MoJ 2012).

The new developments outlined above are intended to produce more opportunities for innovation and creativity in local authorities and the NHS. However, a balance will need to be struck between increased autonomy at a local level to tackle problems and sufficient centralised regulation to identify where local partnerships are failing to adequately protect the most vulnerable children and young people. As the role of Ofsted changes and the emphasis on a different inspection regime across the child protection partnership emerges, LSCBs will be integral to successful multi-agency practice in relation to safeguarding responsibilities. YOT policy and practice must be effectively scrutinised by these bodies when addressing the needs of the most vulnerable young people.

What do we mean by safeguarding?

Effective child protection arrangements require a common understanding of risk between professionals working across criminal justice agencies and children's services. Child protection interventions, sometimes referred to as safeguarding approaches, are statutory procedures which aim to ensure that children are adequately protected from harm, neglect and abuse.[1] Understanding and using an interactive risk perspective will help practitioners – namely frontline staff such as police and probation officers, social workers, health professionals and teachers – to understand the possible effects and risk of harm to children from a wide range of adult behaviour (Kemshall and Wilkinson 2011).

Evidence still shows, when it comes to professional decision-making and assessment of risk, that professionals continue to focus on the individual who is the remit of their service rather than the family (Blyth and Solomon 2012). While there is legislation in place to ensure that wherever there are child protection concerns these override any sensitivities about sharing confidential information regarding adults, too often they are over looked or misunderstood at the frontline. SCRs are local enquiries into the death or serious injury of a child where abuse or neglect is known or suspected to be a factor. Most SCRs, now routinely placed in the public domain, indicate continued problems over the paucity of information sharing between professionals (Brandon *et al* 2010; Davies, 2012; Munro 2011).

Addressing risk in older adolescents

Research tells us that when it comes to sharing information about young people not only do the risk factors become more complex but agencies can also be tardy in information exchange. Older adolescent children are very difficult to help and are often failed by child protection arrangements (Rees *et al* 2011). Risk factors in this age group continue to be:

▶ History of rejection and loss and severe maltreatment (physical, sexual

---

1 The definition provided by HMIP of child protection is the 'ability to demonstrate that all reasonable action has been taken to keep to a minimum the risk of a child or young person coming to harm, either from themselves or from others (ie vulnerability)'.

and neglect, often in combination)

- History of long-term intensive involvement from multiple agencies
- Parents or carers with their own history of abuse and rejection
- Detachment from mainstream schooling
- Pattern of self-harming and self-neglect
- Running away and going missing; evidence of sexual exploitation.

It is the entrenched nature of these risks and the fact that young people may be drawn into other criminal or gang associations that make some cases hard to manage for practitioners working in the youth justice field. The early lives of many adult offenders will have been characterised by these overlapping risk factors and there is strong evidence that exchange of information in relation to safeguarding is not routinely shared with probation and prison staff. Rees *et al* (2011) emphasise that failure to safeguard adolescents can lead to negative outcomes, including cognitive–behavioural deficits, socio-emotional impact and reduced physical health. For YOT practitioners, there is compelling evidence through the YJB effective practice knowledge base of the reduced opportunities for young people in the youth justice system (YJB 2012).

Despite this evidence, it seems that each of the wide-ranging reviews following a child death – in particular those undertaken by Lord Laming in 2003 and 2009 – were influenced by the fact that high-profile tragedies have centred on the deaths of young children. This is certainly the case when considering the impact of the Victoria Climbié case a decade ago and that of Peter Connolly in 2007. Some commentators have noted that developments in policy and practice have been influenced by the aim of preventing similar fatalities and as a result may have overlooked the needs of older adolescents (Rees *et al* 2011). About a quarter of all children who become the subject of a child protection plan in England are aged between ten and 15 years old and Rees *et al* categorically state that maltreated young people in this age group require prompt and targeted support. A recent analysis of SCRs involving death or serious harm to a child or young person found that between a fifth and a quarter of such reviews involved young people aged 11 to 17 years old at the time of the incident (Brandon 2012). In 2011, it was revealed in parliament that a total of 132 young people had died in serious incidents while under supervision in the community since 2006. Serious incidents reports are required by the YJB when a child commits or is a victim of a certain serious specified crime. Further work is required to understand the extent to which serious incident reports flag up safeguarding matters in addition to reviewing critical incidents related to grave crimes.

What does this mean for assessment of risk for YOT practitioners?

Practitioners in YOTs and secure establishments may overlook the fact that risky behaviour by some young people also places them at risk of harm to themselves. Research undertaken by The Children's Society with the University of York states that, while much is known about child maltreatment in this country, far less is understood about how this impacts on adolescents (Rees *et al* 2010). The research concluded that neglect and abuse during teenage years can have just as profound an effect as that in early childhood and will impact on criminal behaviour, substance misuse and health risk behaviours. The findings concluded that practitioners dealt differently with older young people at risk in the following ways:

▶ Young people of ten to 17 were seen as more able to deal with maltreatment, including being able to escape the situation and seek help.

▶ They were perceived by some professionals to be more 'resilient', ie more able to cope with the experiences of maltreatment.

▶ They were more likely to be seen to contribute to and to exacerbate the situation through their own behaviour.

▶ They were seen as putting themselves at risk through risk-taking behaviour such as drinking alcohol and taking drugs.

The study concludes that pursuing multi-agency approaches to supporting young people at risk are fundamental to success; these could include a *Team around the Child* approach or interventions following a multi-agency assessment. For YOT practitioners, any concerns raised in relation to a young person following a youth justice assessment using *Asset* may require follow-through with use of the common assessment framework (CAF). CAF helps practitioners across agencies assess a young person's needs, which should include analysis of risk. Use of CAF allows a common language in relation to need, sets procedures for working together across a local partnership and identifies who will act as a lead professional. Since its inception, over the past decade, there have been difficulties for practitioners using CAF in relating to other established forms of assessment such as *Asset*.

The YJB has consulted on the development of a new Assessment,

Planning and Interventions Framework to take account of other assessment procedures for children in need. This is to be broadly welcomed and may assist YOTs in remaining lead professionals for young people with whom they already have an existing relationship when safeguarding procedures are initiated. The new framework, according to the current YJB website would:

- ❱ Represent a significant shift towards a broader, more comprehensive and needs-based assessment of a child

- ❱ Move away from a narrower focus on criminogenic risk factors

- ❱ Bring youth justice assessment practice closer to the mainstream of children's services

- ❱ Move assessment and intervention planning away from a risk factor-based approach towards a more positive focus that can help reduce the likelihood of offending.

The project underway should ensure closer integration between children's services and YOTs in relation to multi-agency planning. Where authorities operate CAF, YOT workers will be able to act as lead professionals. Evidence suggests that a specialist multi-agency model is most likely to reach the most vulnerable children and young people (Rees *et al* 2011).

In previous research, Rees, alongside Professor Stein from the University of York, highlight areas where professionals feel unclear about the legal position of young people, particularly 16 and 17 year olds in relation to safeguarding (Rees *et al* 2010). It is important that practitioners seek guidance through established YOT policy and make use of multi-agency risk panels where they feel there may be ambiguity about a young person's status as a child or adult. One example of this is in two-way violence and conflict between parents and young people, commonly known as 'parent abuse'. There are few established interventions available to YOTs across the country enabling an effective response to parent abuse (Holt 2012), but it is clear that close liaison between social care agencies, adult services and YOTs provide a means of reconciling very different approaches to resolving a problem.

There remains a paucity of information sharing between probation staff and local authority children's services in relation to the risk that adult offenders may present to children. This reduces the frequency of cases being referred to an appropriate children's professional to assist in the overall protection of the public and joint management of risk of harm. Indeed, it is the cumulative interaction between risk factors that produces the most harmful effects (Brandon *et al* 2010, Davies 2012). Substance misuse, mental illness and domestic abuse are likely to co-exist, and while there is no common risk assessment that can predict serious injury or death, it is important for frontline staff to consider the kinds of responses and working conditions that are likely to manage risk for both children and adults. Ultimately, this requires professionals from different agencies to look beyond their individual specialism and think more broadly to analyse the impact of parental behaviour on children in a household (Action for Children 2011). YOTs are uniquely positioned to straddle information sharing between adult and children's services through Multi Agency Risk Assessment Conferences (MARAC) and Multi Agency Public Protection Arrangements (MAPPA).

Child deaths in England as a result of accident, murder or suicide are relatively rare, though media coverage when they come to public attention may suggest otherwise. Incidents involving adolescents result in less public interest (Family Z: Haringey LSCB 2012). It has to be remembered that the majority of children who have an agreed multidisciplinary child protection plan are generally well served by safeguarding arrangements but older adolescents, often on the edge of the criminal justice system, remain overlooked. Estimates indicate that the total number of violent and maltreatment-related deaths of children and young people under the age of 17 years of age in England is around 85 per year. Of these about 50 to 55 are caused by violence, abuse or neglect and a further 30 to 35 are exacerbated by maltreatment, though those responsible for this research are clear to point out that this is not the primary cause of death (Brandon *et al* 2012).

Of relevance to youth justice practitioners is the fact that adolescents remain one of the two highest risk groups, alongside infants, in relation to fatalities (Brandon *et al* 2012). The need for YOT managers to review the nature and causes of deaths of children and young people on statutory YOT orders is therefore extremely important. The role for LSCBs in holding YOTs and their partners to account in providing services for young people at risk is also paramount.

Child sexual exploitation is another area of child abuse that remains below the radar across statutory services but is increasing in attention, particularly in relation to the children that go missing linked to sexual exploitation. There is growing awareness and intelligence about child trafficking nationally and the importance of information sharing across police, probation and social care services to protect children (DfE 2012; OCC 2012). It is important that all frontline youth justice staff, in YOT and secure settings, are able to identify the early warning signs associated with sexual exploitation.

Existing literature on child sexual exploitation indicates that the proportion of sexually exploited children who are also children in care ranges between 20 and 35 per cent (Jago *et al* 2011; CEOP 2011). Pressure from gangs and groups exacerbates risk of sexual exploitation. It is vital that all frontline staff working with children, young people and adult perpetrators of sexual crimes understand the correlation between children missing, child trafficking and organised crime. This requires a continuing focus on developing a shared understanding about what makes for effective risk of harm practice (HMIP 2011).

Reports published over the summer of 2012 indicate that too often high-risk offenders are placed in geographical areas where there is also a high density of vulnerable children and troubled families (DfE 2012; BBC 2012). Equally important is ensuring that any risk assessment or risk management plan produced by YOT practitioners takes account of the impact of continuing neglect (Rees *et al* 2011). The effect of long-term parental substance misuse, domestic abuse and mental illness on children and young people in terms of outcomes is relatively well documented but less is understood about effective interventions and preventative measures. Safeguarding concerns are not only linked to sexual abuse or physical harm; the number of children who are placed on child protection plans in the category of neglect is higher (Ofsted 2010). For older young people between 10 and 17 years of age, neglect also remains the most common category of maltreatment (Rees *et al* 2011).

In the context of children and young people in the youth justice system, it is important that practitioners do not 'normalise' risky behaviour among adolescents. In assessing safeguarding concerns, staff in YOTs and the secure estate should consider both risk and protective factors and review interventions in the light of wider social, economic and family pressures on the young person.

Analysis of interacting risk factors – the case for multi-agency working

Reflecting the need to focus on public protection and safeguarding work, HMIP provides an analysis of headline scores during inspections. This represents the proportion of risk of harm work in the sample that inspectors rated have been done sufficiently well (HMIP 2011).

Risk of harm in relation to child protection should take account of three key points: the level of vulnerability the young person presents owing to their own behaviour or circumstances; the contact a young person has with other children/peers and the safeguarding issues this raises; and the extent to which the young person remains at risk from adult behaviour. Unfortunately, not all YOT/secure estate practitioners will have liaised with their counterparts in children's services, and despite MAPPA/MARAC arrangements at local level, it cannot be assumed that other relevant statutory agencies covering social care and health have shared information. In the same way that police intelligence is shared across the criminal justice sector, it is vital that police and social care agencies are linked into YOT case management and sentence planning.

For YOT practitioners, risk of harm assessments are routinely integrated into the *Asset* framework. YOTs cannot respond to problems facing adolescents at risk alone and it is important that issues relating to vulnerability and risk are identified during early assessment, planning and review procedures, currently initiated through *Asset*. Any young person considered to be at high risk of harm or of vulnerability is expected to have a risk management plan or vulnerability management plan, produced with referrals to multi-agency support in a set timeframe. These interventions vary, from referral for mental health treatment and support with drug misuse to assistance and information for children at risk of trafficking, gang activity or other forms of sexual exploitation.

Where young people are already subject to a child protection plan or child in need plan through statutory social care arrangements YOT workers must liaise closely with the allocated social worker. Ofsted, in a thematic review of SCRs between 2008 and 2011, found that 18 per cent of all SCRs involved young people over the age of 14 (Ofsted 2011). The cases considered varied enormously but several significant practice issues arose relevant to YOT practitioners in safeguarding young people. The review concluded that practitioners should:

▶ Demonstrate clearly that risk-assessed decision-making informs all actions in relation to older children

▶ Collaborate fully with other agencies working with the young person

▶ Take responsibility for following through any concerns and not assume that someone else is addressing the matter

▶ Challenge other agencies if they have serious concerns that they believe are not being adequately addressed.

It also suggested that LSCBs should:

◗ Carry out audits of complex cases involving older children to identify where agencies are working well together and where improvements can be made and disseminate this learning

◗ Ensure that there are robust mechanisms in place to enable agencies to challenge decision-making processes in relation to safeguarding.

(Ofsted 2011)

Working together to safeguard young people in the youth justice system

The range of services available to YOTs will depend on local guidance related to levels of need. Thresholds, which are in effect the criteria for determining the level of support provided to a young person, may be regarded differently by partner agencies and this can present difficulties for some YOTs in prioritising services. Ultimately, the intervention plan arising from *Asset* should make the case for a co-ordinated and multi-agency set of interventions overseen by the YOT worker.

The challenge of developing new ways of working to promote a more integrated approach across services lies at the heart of legislation since the Victoria Climbié enquiry led by Lord Laming a decade ago. A number of new reforms were set up at a local level under the Children Act 2004 (HM Government 2004). These included children's trusts and Sure Start children's centres as well as new LSCBs in 2006. The *Every Child Matters* guidance attempted to permeate all aspects of work across children's services from 2006 and tried to provide criminal justice agencies, as well as social care, education, health and the voluntary sector, with a thorough grounding in safeguarding, child protection and cohesive concepts of how to best protect children and young people.

With the arrival of the Coalition administration in May 2010, the new government has taken a less centralist stance regarding safeguarding measures and many of these arrangements have been revised over the past two years. Indeed, although some aspects of the *Every Child Matters* doctrine have been retained in some local authority policy and while some areas still operate children's trust partnerships, this is no longer considered a statutory requirement. Local partnerships may have benefited in recent years from strong children's partnerships to support child protection arrangements but they are no longer mandatory. Moreover, any reading of an Ofsted inspection report on safeguarding arrangements at local level in recent years is likely to place emphasis on good partnership and multi-agency policy and practice (Ofsted 2012).

Interestingly, among the changes that the current government administration has introduced, there has been a strengthening of the role of LSCBs, which now have a unique, system-wide role in overseeing child protection arrangements and reporting on progress to improve services for children and young people at local level through an annual report (HM Government 2011). Early in 2012, findings from a survey returned by 57 LSCBs revealed that 86 per cent were positive about developing a child-centred system and enhancing local decision-making about practice and policy. The majority perceived the Munro reforms to create opportunities to move from 'risk averse to risk sensible practice and promote opportunities for frontline workers to exercise their professional judgement' (Munro and Lushey 2012).

The proposed revised *Working Together* framework (HM Government 2012) continues to place a duty of co-operation across statutory partnership agencies in relation to safeguarding. This continues to include YOTs and secure establishments in the children's secure estate. However, the exact representation from youth justice agencies on LSCBs will vary across the country and will increasingly depend on local arrangements. For YOTs and secure establishments, engagement and collaboration with LSCBs are essential.

Multi-agency working in a safeguarding context

YOTs were at the forefront of the development of multi-agency services in the late 1990s, as outlined in the Crime and Disorder Act 1998. Broadly, the model has been considered successful and has led to other multidisciplinary services. Multi-agency working, once synonymous with youth offending services, has become an established model of service delivery. However, despite the promising evidence, there has been limited take up across the system of multi-agency programmes such as multi-systemic therapy (MST) and reconfiguration of services such as that promoted by the multi-agency safeguarding hubs (MASHs) developed in Devon over the past two years (Golden, Aston and Durbin 2011). Even multi-agency training opportunities, demonstrated by the MACIE model, remain under-maximised across the country (Munro 2011).

Multi-agency working varies across the country, but general characteristics include common assessment framework, a focus on information sharing, a mutual understanding of language associated with risk management, and co-location of services and shared governance (Rees *et al* 2011).

Serious case reviews

Following the Munro review (2011), new arrangements for commissioning SCRs have been considered and, at the time of writing, the government is concluding its consultation on how services can best learn lessons from SCRs. In future, each LSCB will be required to devise a learning and knowledge framework and greater emphasis is to be placed on a systems methodology for learning from cases. The most recent biennial review of SCRs was published in July 2012. Key findings are that neglect remains an underlying theme in most SCRs, accounting for 60 per cent (Brandon *et al* 2012). The report also reiterates that neglect is a feature for all ages of children and is as relevant for older adolescents as for young children. The writers conclude that neglect is 'a notable feature in the majority of deaths related to but not directly caused by maltreatment, including sudden unexplained death in infancy (SUDI) and suicide, and in over a quarter of homicides and fatal physical assaults'. Neglect featured in 58 per cent of all non-fatal cases, including physical abuse and sexual abuse.

For YOT practitioners, another key finding of this study is the need for all staff working with young people under the age of 18 to have a good grounding in child development and communication skills. The writers conclude that 'where children have communication impairments the onus is on the professional not the child to find ways of communicating'. As already noted, the voice of young people should be at the centre of YOT work and we know that young people themselves need to be able to contribute effectively to assessments involving risk and vulnerability (Clifton 2012).

The biennial review indicates that there has been a fall in the number of children at the centre of a review with a child protection plan – declining from 16 per cent in 2007/09 to 10 per cent for the most recent two-year period (Brandon *et al* 2012). Since overall numbers of children on child protection plans have risen dramatically over the past three years, this is interesting. YOTs should be encouraged to monitor carefully the numbers of young people on their caseloads who are also subject to child protection planning. Where a young person is then the victim of a serious incident, this should be reported routinely to the LSCB.

Prevention and early intervention

Over the past decade there has been a range of studies aimed at providing an evidence base for early intervention or prevention. The YJB has been at the forefront of policy aimed at developing prevention services in youth justice from 2001 until 2010/11, when the prevention grant allocated to YOTs was no longer ring fenced. Over this decade, different commentators provided much of the evidence on which YOT prevention work has been founded. Recently, Graham Allen, Dame Clare Tickell and Frank Field have all promoted a strong rationale for investment in prevention services to enhance better welfare and educational outcomes for children and young people later in life (Allen 2011; Tickell 2011; Field 2011).

Many YOTs have formed effective projects such as family intervention programmes (FIPs), YISP and YIPs, which were the forerunners for significant prevention work from 2004 onwards, and have developed strong links with family nurse partnerships and parenting programmes at a local level. In recent years, YOTs have formed integrated youth support services (IYSS) as part of local prevention strategies. Government policy has supported the development of Graham Allen's Early Intervention Foundation and, in 2012, the Troubled Families Unit to oversee funding for the most difficult to reach families across the country.

However, despite a recommendation put forward by Munro in 2011, the government has not placed a statutory duty on local authorities to secure the provision of local early help. Similarly, despite two years into the public sector reforms, services have not been reconfigured in the way the Munro review suggests. Local authorities are understandably reluctant to relinquish resources from the most specialist children's services such as child protection, and other partners, such as education, health and policing, are in varying states of flux, which influences their ability to focus on partnership working. Some commentators are concerned that, without strong leadership and a dedicated workforce, the scope for the voluntary and independent sector to pilot innovative new ways of working may be lost. Colin Green, Director of Children's Services in Coventry, argues: 'We need to develop our workforce and enable it to deliver effective early help to address the child or young person's and the family's needs' (Green 2012). He points out that current government policy to expand the Sure Start model, the role of health visiting and the role of the family nurse partnerships is positive but an experienced workforce is 'premium in safeguarding, child protection and public protection work more generally'.

YOTs are well positioned to champion the early offer of help to vulnerable children and young people and their families. It is significant that the Munro review applies the phrase 'early help' to the emergence of problems at any age. Through the 'What do you think?' element of *Asset*, YOT practitioners should be encouraged to respond to young people's safeguarding needs and place any assessment of risk or harm at the centre of any intervention. Office for the Children's Commissioner (OCC 2012) findings suggest that children's experiences are too often not at the heart of actions, decisions or plans. Furthermore, young people may not express their concerns in the terms used by adults (Clifton 2012). The perspectives that Clifton refers to are from consultations led by OCC with children in the child protection system.

> *I don't really think like I'm at risk, it's just a behaviour really, like I don't really feel like I'm in a risky environment or nothings it's just that the things I might say … might trigger things off.*
>
> (Young person, aged 14; Clifton 2012)

Implications for policy and practice in youth justice

The evidence for 'what works' in relation to safeguarding adolescents remains limited. As this chapter has demonstrated, neglect forms a large proportion of child protection cases for children of all ages and a significant number of these will be adolescents (Rees *et al* 2011). Moreover, serious incidents involving young people make up a significant number of SCRs.

For practitioners working in YOTs and the secure estate it is vital that there is a common understanding of risk and need at a local level and that this is shared with other agencies, supported through the LSCB. Any risk assessment framework should be broad and work should be undertaken at national and local policy levels to integrate CAF and *Asset*. Improving good communication, establishing close working relationships and developing a mutual language and definitions of risk between statutory agencies working in youth justice will go a long way to improving services for young people at risk. Co-location of frontline staff, maintaining consistency in relationships with young people and putting the voice of the young person at the centre of any assessment, intervention planning and review framework will also enhance the expertise and skills of practitioners working in youth justice services, in the community and in secure establishments, in relation to safeguarding.

References

Action for Children (2011) *Neglecting the Issue: Impact, Causes and Responses to*

Child Neglect in the UK. London: Action for Children.

Allen G (2011) *Early Intervention: The Next Steps*. London: HM Government.

BBC (2012) *Newsnight*, June 17.

Blyth M (2012) 'Safeguarding and public protection', in M Blom-Cooper (ed) *Learning Lessons in High-risk Cases*. London: NOMS [unpublished].

Blyth M and Solomon E (eds) (2012) *Effective Safeguarding for Children and Young People: What Next After Munro?* Bristol: Policy Press.

Brandon M, Bailey S and Belderson P (2010) *Understanding SCRs and Their Impact: A Biennial Analysis of Serious Case Reviews 2007–9*. London: Department for Children, Schools and Families (DCSF).

Brandon M, Bailey S, Sidebotham P, Belderson P, Hawley C, Ellis C and Megson M (2012) *New Learning from Serious Case Reviews: A Two-year Report from 2009–2011*. London: Department for Education (DfE).

Brewer M, Browne J and Joyce R (2011) *Child and Working-Age Poverty from 2010 to 2020*. London: Institute for Fiscal Studies.

Child Exploitation and Online Protection Centre (CEOP) (2011) *Thematic Assessment. Out of Mind, Out of Sight – Breaking Down the Barriers to Child Sexual Exploitation*. London: CEOP.

Children's Improvement Board (CIB) (2012) *Progress in Implementing the Munro Review of Child Protection and Social Work Reform: A View from the Children's Improvement Board*. London: CIB.

Clifton J (2012) 'The child's voice in the child protection system', in M Blyth and E Solomon (eds) *Effective Safeguarding for Children and Young People: What Next After Munro?* Bristol: Policy Press.

Davies C and Ward H (2012). *Safeguarding Children Across Services: Messages from Research*. London: Jessica Kingsley.

Department for Education (DfE) (2012) *Tackling Child Sexual Exploitation Action Plan: Progress Report*. London: DfE.

Field (2011) *The Foundation Years: Preventing Poor Children Becoming Poor Adults*. London: The Stationery Office.

Golden S, Aston H and Durbin B (2011) *Devon Multi-agency Safeguarding Hub: Case Study Report*. Slough: National Foundation for Educational Research (NFER).

Green C (2012) 'Early intervention', in M Blyth and E Solomon (eds) *Effective Safeguarding for Children and Young People: What next After Munro?*

Bristol: Policy Press.

Haringey LSCB (2012) *Report of the Review of Family Z*. Haringey: LSCB.

HM Government (2004) *The Children Act*. London: The Stationery Office.

HM Government (2010) *Working Together to Safeguard Children: A Guide to Inter-agency Working to Safeguard and Promote the Welfare of Children*. London: DCSF.

HM Government (2011) *Response to Munro*. London: DfE.

HM Government (2012) *Working Together to Safeguard Children. A Consultation*. London: DfE.

HM Inspectorate of Probation (HMIP) (2011) *Annual Report 2010/11*. London: HM Government.

Holt A (2012) 'Adolescent-to-parent abuse and frontline services responses', in M Blyth and E Solomon (eds) *Effective Safeguarding for Children and Young People: What Next After Munro?* Bristol: Policy Press.

Jago S, with Arocha L, Brodie I, Melrose M, Pearce J and Warrington C (2011) *What's Going on to Safeguard Sexually Exploited Young People*. Luton: University of Bedfordshire.

Kelmshall and Wilkinson (2011) *Good Practice in Assessing Risk*. London: Jessica Kingsley.

Munro E (2011) *The Munro Review of Child Protection: Final Report. A Child-centred System*. London: DfE.

Munro E (2012) *Progress Report: Moving Towards a Child-centred System*. London: DfE.

Munro E and Lushey C (2012) *Findings from a National Survey of LSCBs*. Childhood Wellbeing Research Centre.

Office of the Children's Commissioner (OCC) (2012) *Accelerated Report to Secretary of State on the Findings of the OCC Inquiry into Child Sexual Exploitation in Gangs and Groups, with a Special Focus on Children in Care*. London: OCC.

Ofsted (2010) *The Voice of the Child. Learning Lessons from Serious Case Reviews*. London: HM Government.

Ofsted (2011) *Ages of Concern. Learning Lessons from Serious Case Reviews*. London: HM Government.

Ofsted (2012) *Inspection of Safeguarding and Looked after Children Services: Lambeth*. London: HM Government.

Rees G, Gorin S, Jobe A, Stein M, Medford R and Goswami H (2010) 'Executive summary', in *Safeguarding Young People: Responding to Young People aged 11–17 who are Maltreated*. London: The Children's Society.

Rees S, Stein M, Hicks L and Gorvi S (2011) *Adolescent Neglect*. London: Jessica Kingsley.

Tickell C (2011) *Review of Early Years Foundation*. London: HM Government.

Youth Justice Board (YJB) (2012) *Corporate Plan*. London: YJB.

Youth Justice Board and Ministry of Justice (YJB/MoJ) (2012) *Developing the Secure Estate for Children and Young People in England and Wales – Plans until 2015*. London: YJB/MoJ.

3
Custody and resettlement

Rob Allen

Introduction

The vast majority of young people under the age of 18 accused or convicted of criminal offences are dealt with in ways that do not deprive them of their liberty. In certain cases, however, the law allows courts to remand or sentence young people to custody. Young people may find themselves detained for a matter of days awaiting a court appearance or for many years serving a long-term sentence following conviction for a grave crime. However, the numbers involved are relatively small and have fallen sharply since 2008.

Despite small and declining numbers, the use and practice of custodial institutions raise significant questions for youth justice practitioners. At a practical level, the children and young people involved often present particular challenges. This is true for youth offending teams (YOTs) and others working in the community offering alternatives to custody and supervising young offenders on release, and for those responsible for the care of young people in the secure estate.

One challenge arises from the fact that this group includes the most persistent and serious offenders in the country. A recent study undertaken for the Prison Reform Trust (PRT) concluded that 'most of the children who were sentenced to custody were repeat offenders – and it is the persistence rather than the seriousness of the specific offences for which they were sentenced that would seem to explain the use of custody in many or most instances' (Jacobson *et al* 2010). However, at least some of those in custody will have committed serious crimes – at any one time, about one in five are serving long-term sentences for grave crimes (YJB 2010).[1]

Second, many of the youngsters have a range of vulnerabilities caused by entrenched problems experienced at home and at school. In a random sample of 200 young people sentenced to custody, the PRT study found that about half lived in a deprived household or unsuitable accommodation and and just under half had run away from home at some point. Two

---

1   For example, 340 out of 1,690 in June 2012.

fifths were known to have been on the child protection register and/or experienced abuse or neglect and a third had an absent mother. Half had been excluded from school (Jacobsen *et al* 2011).

As a result of their offending and disadvantage, many of these young people prove very demanding to work with, both in the community and in custody. Indeed, around one in five of those sentenced to detention in the latter half of 2008 were imprisoned for breaching conditions of community sentences, antisocial behaviour orders, licences imposed after an earlier release from custody or for failing to surrender to bail (Jacobson *et al* 2010; see also Bateman 2011 and Hart 2011). Some enter custody as a result of a recommendation from the YOT that the courts should take that course of action or, more commonly, in the absence of a proposal for a realistic alternative.

The use of custody for children is a controversial measure, particularly for practitioners who are under a duty to protect and promote the welfare of children. At best, secure establishments provide a safe, structured and caring environment, which can help address the years of neglect, abuse and educational failure that characterise the upbringing of many of the most serious and persistent young offenders. This requires an approach that genuinely meets the needs of individual children in small-scale living units, with intensive preparation for release and continuing care once back in the community. At worst, they can be a frightening interlude in young lives already impoverished by neglect and punishment. Even smaller closed institutions in the local authority or secure training sector struggle to overcome the hostility and alienation felt by many of the children detained against their will. After all, closed institutions of whatever kind represent an abnormal living experience, which can impair the normal course of adolescent development. Whatever the intentions of the law, policymakers and staff, concentrating highly delinquent young people in a closed environment risks reinforcing rather than weakening the attitudes the justice system is seeking to challenge. The common use of physical restraint in custodial establishments may further contribute to an 'us and them' attitude towards authority. The incidence of self-harm and even deaths – there were three deaths in juvenile custody in 2011/12 – illustrate the vulnerability of those in custody.

Equipping residents to lead more positive lives is also an uphill task without intensive follow-up support and a willingness on the part of schools, social workers and employers to give the young people a chance on release. It is perhaps not surprising that the results in terms of reoffending for all forms of custody have remained stubbornly high, with four out of every five young people back before the courts within two years.

This chapter summarises what the research tells us about the use and practice of custodial institutions. Section A describes the institutions that make up the secure estate and recent trends in their use. Section B explains the norms that govern the use and practice of custody and the findings of recent research studies. Section C proposes what can be done to keep the numbers of children and young people in custody to a minimum, and Section D sets out what should be done in custody and afterwards for those young people who are locked up. Section E offers examples of approaches that are used in a number of European countries and Section F some concluding remarks.

Section A
What is custody?

Custodial establishments for juveniles fall broadly into three categories. Young offender institutions (YOIs), which form part of the prison service, accommodate the overwhelming majority of young people in custody: 76 per cent in June 2012. Secure children's homes (SCHs), largely run by local authorities nowadays, take fewer than 10 per cent of those in custody; and secure training centres (STCs), run by private companies, detained about 15 per cent of the juvenile custody population in June 2012.

A recent change to the law enables the Secretary of State to specify additional forms of accommodation where young people serving a Detention and Training Order (DTO) may be placed, but the provision has yet to be implemented.[2] There are also small numbers of young people held in secure accommodation in the health system whose costs are met by the NHS. But the vast majority of those under 18 in custody are held in YOIs, SCHs and STCs, and of these more than three quarters are in YOIs.

Since 2000, the Youth Justice Board (YJB) has been responsible for commissioning and purchasing secure places for under 18 year olds remanded and sentenced to custody by the courts. In 2011/12, it spent £245.5m on the purchase of secure places – 62 per cent of its total budget.

At the time of writing, there are ten YOIs taking under 18s. Of the seven male establishments, five are dedicated to the juvenile age range, with capacities ranging from 157 (Cookham Wood) to 440 (Hindley). One, Ashfield, is privately run. The other two institutions are Feltham, where 240 under 18 year olds are accommodated on the same site but separately from 500 young adults, and Parc, a private prison in Wales, where a juvenile unit

---

2 Offender Management Act 2007, section 34.

for 60 under 18s is situated in what is primarily an adult establishment. All three YOIs taking young women under 18 accommodate them in juvenile units that form part of adult prisons. The average cost for a place in a YOI in April 2012 was £60,000 per year.

The YJB has been responsible for overseeing the contracts for the four STCs since 1 April 2000. The average annual cost of an STC place, excluding VAT, has risen steadily, from £132,000 in 2000/01 to £178,000 in 2012/13. The YJB does not set precise staff to prisoner ratios for STCs; instead, it agrees with providers the minimum starting levels necessary to ensure effective supervision. Broadly speaking, minimum staffing levels are three members of custody staff to young people living in a group of eight, and two members of custody staff to young people living in a group of six. It is estimated that 11 per cent of the costs are spent on education.

In 2012, the YJB contracted with 10 SCHs, which are run by local authorities and subject to licensing and inspection by the Department for Education. Recent inspection reports by the Commission for Social Care Inspectorate have been very positive but, as a consequence of having the highest staffing ratios, the units are the most expensive in the estate, with an annual cost per place of £212,000. SCHs play an important role in providing secure care for children who are not necessarily offenders but who need to be locked up for their own protection – often very vulnerable children who run away from other placements. Local authority demand for welfare places has fallen in recent years, contributing to the closure of several units. At 31 March 2012, there were 300 approved places in 17 units in England and Wales, a reduction of 50 places since 2003. Ten years earlier there were 445 approved places in 32 secure units.

Trends in the use of custody

In June 2012, there were, on average, 1,619 juveniles in custody (MoJ 2012). During the course of the 2010/11 financial year, a total of 4,177 custodial sentences were imposed on under 18 year olds, which represents less than one in every 1,000 young people in the ten to 17 age range (YJB/MoJ 2012). During the same year, young people were remanded to custody on 3,485 occasions. Significantly larger numbers are detained overnight in police cells – more than 50,000 aged 16 and under in the two years 2008 and 2009.[3] While this can be a distressing experience for children, it is at least a short one, with the vast majority released into the community promptly.

---

3   17 year olds are treated as adults; figures from Howard League 2011.

The number of children under 18 who are imprisoned in England and Wales has fallen by more than a third over the last four years, from about 3,000 in the first half of 2008 to less than 2,000 in the first part of 2012. This unexpected fall represents the largest decline in custody for children since the 1980s (Allen 2011; Bateman 2012). The sharp reduction does not reflect a broader trend in the use of custody, which has risen for adults over the same period, but has been largely brought about by fewer children being sentenced to DTOs, with particularly marked declines in the numbers of younger children and girls. Declines have been particularly marked in large conurbations. The falls do not apply as much to black and minority ethnic children as to white. A number of factors explain the fall, but it is not the case that reducing custody has been a deliberate or overt policy objective in central government. Rather, a number of factors behind the scenes have worked together to reduce the number of children appearing before the courts, reducing the proportion of these children who are sentenced to custody.

Responsibility for youth justice in government transferred from the Home Office to the Ministry of Justice (MoJ) and Department for Children, Schools and Families (DCSF) in 2007, and local authorities were required to pay greater attention to meeting the needs of children in conflict with the law. Incentives for the police to bring minor cases into the system were removed and as a result informal and constructive responses were developed. This has led to a marked fall in the number of first-time entrants to the youth justice system, although the extent to which this represents a change in crime levels or a change in the way children are dealt with, in particular by the police, is difficult to disentangle. The overall level of crime as a whole, and of serious youth violence, declined across the country between 2008 and 2010. It is worth noting that the reduction in the child custodial population appears to have been achieved without prompting any increase in youth crime.

The number of children appearing in court has fallen by almost a quarter since 2008 but, despite dealing with smaller numbers of more serious and persistent cases, the courts have sentenced a smaller percentage of them to custody. These falls in custody may to an extent reflect the impact of legislative changes in the Criminal Justice and Immigration Act 2008 and a constructive guideline published by the Sentencing Guidelines Council (SGC) but started well before these came into effect at the end of 2009. There is some evidence of a greater engagement between the YJB and YOTs on the one hand and the courts on the other which may have developed a shared view that custody should be a last resort. Outside the system, initiatives such as the PRT's *Out of Trouble* campaign have developed innovative ways of raising awareness of the use of custody for children nationally and locally and have provided technical assistance in areas with high rates of custodial sentencing.

While it is difficult to assess its impact, it appears that the climate of political, media and public opinion has not led to demands for a greater use of custody during this period. Prior to the publication of the Legal Aid, Sentencing and Punishment of Offenders Bill in June 2011, there was a considerable backlash against what was portrayed in parts of the media as an unduly soft approach to sentencing by the Coalition government. The backlash, and the changes in policy which resulted, have by and large not applied to measures for the ten to 17 age range. The serious disturbances in towns and cities across England in August 2011 do not appear to have impacted on the sentencing climate either, other than by creating a short-lived spike in numbers remanded and sentenced to custody in the immediate aftermath.

Section B
International and national norms

The UN Convention on the Rights of the Child (UN 1990a) makes it clear that locking up children should be a measure of last resort and for the shortest possible time. It also requires institutions to be educational in nature, with more detailed guidance provided in the Havana Rules (UN 1990b). The Council of Europe's Rules for Juvenile Offenders Subject to Sanctions or Measures sets out more detailed requirements for custodial establishments pointing out, *inter alia*, that 'all staff working with juveniles perform an important public service. Their recruitment, special training and conditions of work shall ensure that they are able to provide the appropriate standard of care to meet the distinctive needs of juveniles and provide positive role models for them' (Council of Europe 2008).

It is clear that the custodial estate in England and Wales fails to meet many of the requirements of these international norms. The basic range and structure of the secure estate and of the custodial institutions that comprise it are in large part unsuitable for the task. The Council of Europe is clear that life in an institution should approximate as closely as possible the positive aspects of life in the community; that numbers of juveniles in an institution should be small enough to enable individualised care; and that institutions should be organised into small living units. Furthermore, juvenile institutions should be located in places that are easy to access, facilitate contact between the juveniles and their families, and provide conditions with the least restrictive security and control arrangements necessary to protect juveniles from harming themselves, staff, others or the wider community.

For the most part, YOIs, where the overwhelming majority of young offenders are held, fall far short on all of these fronts. With the exception of particular units with special funding and arrangements – for example Wetherby's Keppel unit for vulnerable juveniles[4] – the prison service is simply unable to provide the kind of buildings, staffing levels or regimes to provide the kind of individualised, therapeutic approach required by the rules.

The gap between the philosophy of the European rules and what is provided in England and Wales is perhaps best illustrated by examples relating to the provision of education and the issue of discipline. The rules say: 'As far as possible arrangements shall be made for juveniles to attend local schools and training centres and other activities in the community' (rule 78.2). This is something that seldom if ever happens in the custodial estate. As far as disciplinary measures are concerned, the European rules state that only conduct likely to constitute a threat to good order, safety or security may be defined as a disciplinary offence and that disciplinary procedures shall be mechanisms of last resort: 'Restorative conflict resolution and educational interaction with the aim of norm validation shall be given priority over formal disciplinary hearings and punishments' (rule 94.1). By way of contrast, the Chief Inspector of Prisons noted in his latest annual report that, in its annual survey, '58 per cent of young men and 30 per cent of young women reported that they had had adjudication. Some charges were due to minor infringements of rules or childish behaviour and could have been dealt with differently' (HMI 2011a).

There is a marked contrast too between what goes on in custodial establishments – particularly YOIs – and the types of approach recommended to promote the quality of life of looked after children. It was estimated in 2011 that about 400 young people in custody might have spent time in care; under the Legal Aid Sentencing and Punishment of Offenders Act, all children remanded into detention are to be treated as looked after (HMI 2011b).

Guidance on the treatment of looked after children emphasises measures that 'put the voices of children, young people and their families at the

---

4   According to an inspection report in 2012, 'The living conditions were still good and staff cared for young people with a great deal of sensitivity, were appreciative of their different needs, and provided a high level of individual support. The unit continued to be a busy and purposeful place and young people who were discharged to their communities were well prepared for release.'

heart of service design and delivery' and 'encourage warm and caring relationships between child and carer that nurture attachment and create a sense of belonging so that the child or young person feels safe, valued and protected' (NICE 2010). Recent inspections have found that young people spent too much time locked up during their induction and this contributed to their overall feelings of being unsafe (Feltham); that staff admitted they did not always respond to bullying because the formal systems were too complex (Warren Hill); and that the lack of staff engagement with young people continued to be a problem and managers felt this often stemmed from a lack of confidence in some staff in dealing with difficult situations (Ashfield). As for families, at Wetherby, many young people were held a long distance from their homes and facilities for visitors were poor: 'Few young people got frequent family visits and there was no monitoring of family contact to identify whether maintaining contact with family and friends was a problem to be addressed' (HMI 2012). A broader review of the whole secure estate in 2010 found that families attended approximately 50 per cent of training planning review meetings and 'very little action was taken to try to increase their attendance' (HMI 2010). The structural nature of many of these shortcomings suggests that practitioners should be doing what they can to keep the number of children in custody to an absolute minimum.

Section C
Using custody as a last resort

The use of custody varies between regions and between local authority areas. In 2010/11, one in 636 ten to 17 year olds received a custodial sentence in London compared to one in 2,380 in South West England. Only one of 12,500 young people in Bracknell Forest was sent to custody, compared to one in every 268 in Lambeth. Although differing levels of crime and of young offenders explains much of the variation, boroughs with similar offending profiles use custody very differently. In 2010/11, 59 young people from Southwark went to custody compared to 23 in Tower Hamlets, 45 from Rochdale compared to 28 from Oldham (MoJ/YJB 2011).

Research indicates a range of measure that practitioners can take to help reduce the use of custody for juveniles and to keep it at a low level. These include: working to bring about a high level of diversion from court by encouraging informal action as well as reprimands and final warnings; proposing that courts make use of the full range of low-level penalties, including conditional discharges, when young people first appear in court; and making sparing use of Supervision Orders with additional requirements, reserving these for young people who are genuinely at risk of a custodial sentence. Such tariff management strategies can serve to delay the progression of young people through the court system so that they have greater opportunities to turn away from delinquency. Also, even if they continue offending, courts may take longer to reach the view that there is no alternative to custody (Bateman and Stanley 2002).

Intervening promptly in respect of young people at risk of being remanded to custody through the provision of suitable bail programmes in appropriate cases is also important, as is the range and quality of services made available more broadly by the YOT to form part of a package of non-custodial measures. How effective such packages are at dissuading courts from remanding or sentencing young people to custody depends on the relationship between the YOT and the court and on the quality of the communications between the two, most commonly in the form of the pre-sentence report.

Research on the attitudes of sentencers has found them to be generally sceptical about the effectiveness of custody as a means of preventing reoffending by young people (Solanki and Utting 2009). Sentencers argue that custody fails to address the underlying causes of offending behaviour, does more harm than good, risking making 'bad people worse', and has little impact on individual deterrence, as evidenced by the high rates of reoffending. In so far as custody is deemed effective, this chiefly relates to taking young offenders out of circulation for the time that they are imprisoned, allowing the community a period of respite. Despite general scepticism about the value of custody, the research also found that 'there was a widespread and strongly held view among sentencers that custodial sentences were given to young offenders because they had become 'unavoidable'. This endpoint could be reached because of the seriousness of an offence, but more commonly sentencers described feeling that community alternatives had been exhausted and 'enough was enough'.

Clearly, engaging with the court's specific concerns about the risks and characteristics of individual young offenders is important in keeping them out of custody. At a practical level, this requires the attendance of practitioners at court. In Solanki and Utting's (2009) research, 'There was general satisfaction expressed with the quality and commitment of YOT staff. However, some sentencers complained that the level of attendance by YOT officers in their courts was unsatisfactory. This was attributed to financial and staffing shortages.'

Familiarity with the legal provisions governing the use of custody is obviously a prerequisite for effective work in this area. The Legal Aid Sentencing and Punishment of Offenders Act 2012 creates new custodial remand provisions for under 18s who are charged with or convicted of a criminal offence or concerned in extradition proceedings. It repeals the existing framework set out in the Children and Young Persons Act 1969 and removes provisions under which 17 year olds are currently remanded in prison. Once implemented, the law will make provision for all under 18s who have been refused bail to be remanded in custody according to the same tests. It removes the existing distinctions based on age and gender and imposes a more rigorous test before under 18s can be remanded to youth detention accommodation (www.legislation.gov.uk/ukpga/2012/10/section/109).

For custodial sentences, the law has long prohibited courts from passing such disposals unless it is of the opinion that the offending is so serious that neither a fine alone nor a community sentence can be justified for the offence (Criminal Justice Act 2003, s152(2)). New provisions in the Criminal Justice and Immigration Act 2008 specifically require the court, before sentencing a child to custody, to 'state its reasons for being satisfied that the offence(s) is (are) so serious that no other sanction is appropriate and, in particular, why a youth rehabilitation order with intensive supervision and surveillance or with fostering cannot be justified' (SGC 2009).

There is much useful material contained in the definitive guidelines on the sentencing of youths published by the SGC (2009). These highlight a number of legislative and non-legislative reasons for restricting the use of custody. For example: under both domestic law and international convention, a custodial sentence must be imposed only as a 'measure of last resort' (which is not strictly the case in the case of domestic law); the custody threshold is higher in the case of a child than in the case of an adult; and it is clear that parliament expects custodial sentences to be imposed only rarely on those aged 14 or less. For all children aged ten to 17, where the offence has crossed the custody threshold, the statutory tests are likely to be satisfied only where a custodial sentence will be more effective in preventing offending. The guidance points out that the obligation to have regard to the welfare of the offender requires a court to take account of a wide range of issues, including those relating to mental health, capability and maturity, and that they must be alert to welfare needs and the vulnerability of children to self-harm, particularly in a custodial environment. It also includes a range of technical matters that help restrict the use of custody: for example, a sentence that follows reoffending does not need to be more severe than the previous sentence solely because there has been a previous conviction; even where the custody threshold has been crossed, a court is not required to impose a custodial sentence; and before imposing a custodial sentence as a result of re-sentencing following breach, a court should be satisfied that the YOT and other local authority services have taken all steps necessary to ensure that the child has been given the appropriate opportunity and support necessary for compliance. Reducing the numbers entering custody for breach is one of the challenges facing practitioners in the future.

Section D
Good practice in custody

When considering what can be done to ensure that any custodial experience for a juvenile makes it less rather than more likely that they will reoffend, it is all too easy to overlook the significance of addressing some of the basic quality of life issues with which many custodial establishments struggle. As the YJB has recognised, 'reoffending can only be addressed in a safe, secure environment. Effective safeguarding is therefore important not only in its own right, but also because it is critical to reducing reoffending' (MoJ/YJB 2012).

Troublingly, recent inspection reports show that custodial institutions have problems in meeting some of the very basic needs of juveniles, let alone producing more positive outcomes. The Chief Inspector of Prisons reported in 2010/11: 'In three establishments, external nutritionists had been consulted but young men said they frequently felt hungry' (HMI 2011a). At Feltham, in 2011, 'many areas of the establishment had poor standards of cleanliness, including residential units and cells, the grounds, the Wren unit, the segregation unit and health care' (HMI 2011d). At Wetherby, there was inadequate access to showers, with the lack of daily showers particularly affecting those who worked in dirty areas (HMI 2012).

Surveys conducted by the Inspectorate have found just under a third of young men and just over a fifth of young women in YOIs reporting that they had felt unsafe at some point while in prison. In 2009, inspectors described Cookham Wood as frightening and unsafe. In most establishments, the use of force by staff to control young people is frequent and, in some, bullying between young people is a serious problem. An inspection at Feltham conducted after the 2011 riots found 'the introduction of some young people to gangs and a violent culture in prison, which they had not previously experienced' (HMI 2011c).

Some of the practices undertaken in custody such as routine strip-searching are seen by some observers to raise questions of decency (National Council for Independent Monitoring Boards 2011) and by the Chief Inspector of Prisons to mar efforts by reception staff to reassure new arrivals for whom arriving in custody is 'a daunting experience'. While the inspectors found that most young people said that staff treated them with respect (69 per cent of young men and 81 per cent of young women), young men from black and minority ethnic groups reported less favourably: only 57 per cent said they were treated respectfully. The Chief Inspector noted: 'Some young people were very negative about the way they were treated' (HMI 2011a).

It should go without saying that efforts to influence young people to stay out of trouble in the future are likely to be ineffective in institutional environments where some young people do not have enough to eat, cannot keep themselves clean, do not feel safe and are not treated with respect. But more direct attempts to bring about changes in attitudes and behaviour by young people in custody have also been disappointing. Inspectors found that 'support from personal officers/key workers was generally not rated highly by young people. Sixty-seven per cent of young women said that a member of staff had checked on them within the previous week to see how they were getting on, but for young men this dropped to 39%' (HMI 2011a). Few personal officers attended important meetings relating to the care of the young people for whom they were responsible. While the overall care of the most vulnerable and troublesome young people, including those who self-harmed or were segregated, had improved and most establishments had a multi-agency forum in which they discussed individual young people and shared information, the co-ordination of a wide range of assessments and care plans for different purposes was poor, resulting in a disjointed approach to caring for the most challenging young people. At Wetherby, the separation and care unit was a bleak environment and the regime and individual care plans for the most problematic young people were poor (HMI 2012). At Feltham, 'a high number of young people were regularly excluded from education or refused to attend and many classes had been cancelled' (HMI 2011d).

Particular groups of young people suffer more than others. YOIs have experienced difficulties in identifying, assessing and managing the needs of looked after children without social work expertise to help them interpret relevant legislation and guidance and to ensure that the needs of looked after children are met. At Feltham, the provision for foreign nationals (almost a quarter of those in the establishment as a whole) was poor on all levels. Cookham Wood had a significant number of Travellers and little work had been done to address their specific needs. Further work was also needed in relation to young people with disabilities. There was a failure to identify which young people had learning difficulties or disabilities, yet this could have a significant impact on their experience of custody.

The most important lesson about custodial care relates to the need to meet these basic and specific needs before seeking to apply more ambitious programme interventions that aim to produce changes in behaviour and attitude. While it is tempting to want to identify interventions which stop offenders leaving prison from committing crime, the most recent criminological evidence suggests that treatment must take into account the human processes and social contexts through which change happens, and the meaning offenders attach to the efforts being made to reintegrate them. It has been argued that the 'what works' approach should be replaced by a new 'desistance paradigm', which aims to focus on opportunities and motivations, and to help ex-offenders discover their capacity to make and enact choices in order to resist and overcome pressures that may lead them back to crime (McNeill 2006). This is highly relevant to work with young offenders in custody. The paradigm suggests that a casework approach should be applied by YOTs and practitioners in the secure estate to their work with young people and attaches priority to the need to engage effectively with young offenders' families, to enlist their support where possible in helping offenders to change their ways.

Thus one important finding from research is to emphasise processes of change – how to work with young people – rather than simply identify modes of intervention – what to do with them. A second is that interventions should not necessarily be concerned *solely* with preventing further offending. Encouraging offenders to make amends to victims and to communities through restorative processes and community service can play a part in convincing them that they are managing to become a different person – an essential component of sustained desistance from crime.

Maguire (2007) has identified a number of basic tenets which seem significant for work on custody and resettlement:

a) Individuals differ in their readiness to change

b) Motivation is the key to change

c) Desistance is a long process, with relapses – zig zagging

d) Overcoming social problems may be necessary but is not sufficient to promote desistance

e) As people change, they need new skills and opportunities.

Alongside this desistance paradigm, it is important to consider elements of compliance or procedural justice theory, which argue that justice agencies will only command compliance from offenders if they treat them in a way that is transparently fair. Negotiating a shared agenda for change is likely to produce better results than imposing one.

The principle of so called 'responsivity' – that different offenders have different learning styles and that work should be tailored to these – is also important. This may be particularly significant in relation to any role played by the police in post-release supervision. Evidence from prolific and other priority offender (PPO) schemes suggests that there can be dissonance between the approach of the police and other partners, underpinned by confusion about the overall aims of the project. From the point of view of some offenders, it is possible that police involvement may be a disincentive to participate in any programme. For others, the key factor will be whether reliable and relevant help is provided, whoever is providing it.

While there is limited evidence about effectiveness, many offenders say that they would prefer to receive help from people who have been through the criminal justice and prison system themselves. Evidence shows the kind of casework approach that is likely to prove most successful. What has been called 'core correctional practice' includes:

▶ Effective use of authority

▶ Pro-social modelling and reinforcement

▶ Problem solving

▶ Open, warm, empathetic and enthusiastic attitudes.

Lessons from Resettlement Pathfinders in the past decade suggest that models based around three elements are most likely to produce positive effects: motivational and other work prior to release, post-release mentoring, and facilitating access to agencies and organisations (Lewis *et al* 2003). Meeting basic practical needs remains crucial. The Prison Inspectorate has reported that 'barriers such as not having a suitable address, a lack of appropriate courses and not being able to start courses immediately after release meant that many young people did not have an education or training placement to attend and of those that did, few were able to sustain it. A large number of young people had concerns about finding somewhere to live. Resettlement teams identified accommodation problems early, but often accommodation for young people not returning to their families was only confirmed very late in their sentence' (HMI 2011). A Prison Inspectorate review of training plans for children and young people (HMI 2010) noted that arrangements for reviewing their progress while in custody were hampered by inadequate targets, infrequent meetings, variable attendance by key contributors and even a lack of appropriate locations for the discussions. In a survey conducted for a thematic inspection report on resettlement provision for children and young people, only a third of young men had an education training or employment place arranged on release, only half were still attending a month later, and only a fifth of those who had not got a placement on release had one confirmed month later: 'Overall the outcomes for our sample were very disappointing' (HMI 2011e).

Even in secure units and secure training centres, where staffing is much more generous, an Ofsted (2010) review found that agreed discharge arrangements for young people were commonly not in place until the last days of the placement: 'Social workers and workers from youth offending teams did not participate sufficiently in planning for young people to move back into the community. Staff in secure placements were usually unable to make significant continuing contributions to planning or services for young people after they were discharged.'

Section E
Approaches in Europe

In a survey conducted by the Council of Europe (2008) as part of its work to develop rules on juvenile sanctions, many countries identified reintegration as a core purpose alongside education, normalisation and preventing the negative effects of deprivation of liberty. This is particularly true of institutions located in child welfare departments, where regimes can more easily enable young people to maintain links with their families and communities through periods of supervised and unsupervised leave. In German welfare institutions, step-by-step plans are developed 'according to which juveniles may be given additional leave after several weeks if they comply with the rules. Most facilities with deprivation of liberty impose a ban on leaving and contact in the first few weeks (exception: correspondence by letter). More and more contacts are possible as the deprivation of liberty is relaxed, ranging as far as free-time home visits' (Council of Europe 2008).

At the Etablissements Pénitentiaires pour Mineurs in France, weekly reports to parents are made outlining progress and challenges. The Folch i Torres Educational Centre outside Barcelona has no restrictions on family members visiting in normal working hours. The Finnish Child Welfare Act (section 34) provides special aftercare for juveniles when released from a welfare institution, which also involves also work with the parents or legal guardians (if needed, until the juvenile reaches the age of 21). In Slovakia and Switzerland, parents are specially integrated in joint activities including parents groups.

Specific measures to prepare for release are made at the so-called 'reso' units in the Amsterdam detention centre, or JOC, for the boys who are about to leave. With the approval of the youth judge or the public prosecutor, boys are allowed to go to school or work outside the JOC. Educational and training programmes are provided to make the transition back to society easier. In Germany, a major inquiry following the death of a young prisoner at Siegburg recommended that North-Rhine Westphalia should implement more open sections in detention for juveniles, to reduce the potential of inter-prisoner violence and to help prepare young people for release (Allen 2009). Working outside the institution is allowed in Austria, and Switzerland clarified that only very few places exist in a closed setting and that in these institutions a similar phase model is applied, with increasing contacts and periods of leave over the time. In Sweden, a guiding principle is the focus on reintegration and normalisation, and the institutions work to establish pro-social activities. For example, the young person can attend the community school close to the institution and can have long-term visits to family and leave.

In Catalonia's juvenile justice centres, the Law of Penal Responsibility of Minors 2000 establishes the clear objective of social inclusion, which applies to all the professionals working in the system. Measures of deprivation of liberty are divided into two parts along the lines of the DTO in England and Wales. The first part is deprivation of liberty itself and the second is a proportionate period of supervised freedom by a social educator. The institutions use individual leave periods as a way of preparation for release (with the judge's agreement). The leave has specific aims (renewing documentation, family reunification, job interview, etc). Professionals prepare for the leave with the juvenile and with his or her family. At first periods of leave are brief and they then become longer, step-by-step, if the juvenile fulfils the agreements. A mentor supervises the operation of this programme.

In Catalonia there are three specific open centres for juveniles (usually those without a family or a positive family). If a juvenile in a closed institution makes good progress, the institution can ask the judge to allow an open placement and moves the juvenile to one of the centres – effectively small flats in the community with support from a team of educators. Catalonia also has a specific public enterprise working for work insertion and work training of juvenile and adult inmates.

In establishments that form part of the prison system, maintaining contacts are less of a priority across Europe, but there are exceptions. In Norway, apart from the principle of allocating juveniles close to their homes, section 3 of the Execution of Sentences Act 2001 stipulates that particular importance must be attached to a child's right of access to his or her parents during the execution of a sanction. Many countries claim that outside agencies are involved in helping prepare young offenders for release, including Denmark, Finland, France, Germany (reinforced by the juvenile penitentiary laws of 2008), Hungary, Italy, Latvia, Lithuania, Norway, Portugal, Scotland, Slovakia, Spain, Sweden, Switzerland and Ukraine.

Section F
Conclusions

There are a number of ways of building on the success achieved in reducing the number of children in custody in England and Wales in the future. The most obvious challenge is to reduce the use of custodial remands. The Legal Aid, Sentencing and Punishment of Offenders Act 2012 introduces a new legal framework for the remand of all those under 18 to custody. This should result in fewer 17 year olds (who are currently subject to adult remand provisions) being held in custody awaiting trial and offers the opportunity for reductions in younger children too. There is work to do too in trying to reduce the numbers who end up in custody having breached the requirements of community-based orders, to divert into more appropriate accommodation children with mental health problems and learning disabilities, and to address the disproportionate use of custody for black and minority ethnic children.

As for what happens in custody, it is a sobering finding from the Prison Inspectorate that, although 91 per cent of young men and 97 per cent of young women said that they wanted to stop offending on release, fewer than half felt that they had done something in custody to make them less likely to offend in future. Addressing basic expectations in custody must remain a priority – time out of cell, daily exercise and association, education and training. Maintaining contact with families and the outside world is a basic prerequisite for successful resettlement. Surveys conducted by the Prison Inspectorate in 2010/11 found that 30 per cent of young men and 47 per cent of young women said they had had no visits in the last month or had never had a visit (HMI 2011a).

On resettlement itself, good practice depends on the willingness and ability of agencies outside the criminal justice and social care systems to give priority to a needy but demanding group. Apart from the squeeze on resources facing many of these agencies, the government has proposed changes to the legal framework that currently protect the assessment of vulnerable children in need, including those being released from custody with nowhere to live and no support. The broader picture needs to take account of the way young people effect their transition to adulthood and how well the criminal justice agencies – YOTs, the probation and prison services – assist that process. This is an area that is receiving belated attention thanks in part to the work of the T2A Alliance (see Allen 2012).

References

Allen R (2009) 'Custodial establishments for juveniles in Europe', in Junger, Tas and Dunkel (eds) *Reforming Juvenile Justice*. Springer.

Allen R (2011) *Last Resort: Exploring the Reduction in Child Imprisonment 2008–11*. London: Prison Reform Trust (PRT).

Allen (2012) 'Young adults in the English criminal justice system', in LF Bottoms and FD Young (eds) *Young Adult Offenders Lost in Transition?* Abingdon: Routledge.

Bateman T (2011) 'We now breach more kids in a week than we used to in a whole year: the punitive turn, enforcement and custody', *Youth Justice*, 11(2): 115–133.

Bateman T (2012) 'Who pulled the plug on youth justice', *Youth Justice*, 12: 136–152.

Bateman T and Stanley C (2002) *Patterns of Sentencing: Differential Sentencing across England and Wales*. London: Youth Justice Board (YJB).

Council of Europe (2008) 'Recommendation CM/Rec 11 of the Committee of Ministers to member states on the European Rules for juvenile offenders subject to sanctions or measures'. Available at: https://wcd.coe.int/ViewDoc.jsp?id=1367113&Site=CM&BackColorInternet=C3C3C3&BackColorIntranet=EDB021&BackColorLogged=F5D383

Hart D (2011) *Into the Breach*. London: PRT.

HMI (2010) *Prison Inspectorate Thematic Report: Training Planning for Children and Young People*. Available at: www.justice.gov.uk/downloads/publications/inspectorate-reports/hmipris/thematic-reports-and-research-publications/Training_Planning_Thematic_rps.pdf

HMI (2011a) *HM Chief Inspector of Prisons for England and Wales Annual Report, 2010/11*. Available at: www.justice.gov.uk/downloads/publications/corporate-reports/hmi-prisons/hmip-annual-report-2010-11.pdf

HMI (2011b) *The Care of Looked After Children in Custody: A Short Thematic Review* (May). Available at: www.justice.gov.uk/downloads/publications/inspectorate-reports/hmipris/thematic-reports-and-research-publications/looked-after-children-2011.pdf

HMI (2011c) 'Update to the report of the unannounced full follow-up inspection in July 2011 of HMYOI Feltham (young people under 18)'. Available at: www.justice.gov.uk/downloads/publications/inspectorate-reports/hmipris/prison-and-yoi-inspections/feltham/feltham-health-check-2011.pdf

HMI (2011d) 'Report on an unannounced full follow-up inspection of HMYOI Feltham (young people under 18), 18– 22 July 2011'. Available at: www.justice.gov.uk/downloads/publications/inspectorate-reports/hmipris/prison-and-yoi-inspections/feltham/feltham2011.pdf

HMI (2011e) 'Resettlement provision for children and young people'. Available at: www.justice.gov.uk/downloads/publications/inspectorate-reports/hmipris/thematic-reports-and-research-publications/Resettlement-thematic-june2011.pdf

HMI (2012) 'Report on an announced inspection of HMYOI Wetherby, 30 January–3 February 2012'. Available at: www.justice.gov.uk/downloads/publications/inspectorate-reports/hmipris/prison-and-yoi-inspections/wetherby/wetherby-2012.pdf

Jacobson J, Bhardwa B, Gyateng T, Hunter G and Hough M (2010) *Punishing Disadvantage: A Profile of Children in Custody*. London: PRT.

Lewis S, Vennard J, Maguire M, Raynor P, Vanstone M, Raybould S and Rix A (2003) *The Resettlement of Short-term Prisoners: An Evaluation of Seven Pathfinder Programmes*. London: Home Office.

McNeill F (2006) 'A desistance paradigm for offender management', *Criminology and Criminal Justice*, 6(1): 39–61.

Maguire M (2007) 'The resettlement of ex prisoners', in L Gelsthorpe and R Morgan (eds) *The Handbook of Probation*. Uffculme: Willan.

MOJ (2012) *Monthly Data and Analysis Report*, June. Available at: www.justice.gov.uk/statistics/youth-justice/custody-data

MoJ/YJB (2011) 'Regional data: use of custody regionally 2010–11'. Available at: www.justice.gov.uk/statistics/youth-justice/statistics

MoJ/YJB (2012) *Developing the Secure Estate for Children and Young People in England and Wales*: Plans until 2015: para 21.

National Council for Independent Monitoring Boards (2011) *Behind Closed Doors: Annual Report 2011*. Available at: www.justice.gov.uk/downloads/about/imb/imb-national-council-annual-report-2011.pdf

NICE (2010) *Promoting the Quality of Life of Looked-after Children and Young People*.

Ofsted (2010) *Admission and Discharge from Secure Accommodation*. Manchester. Available at: www.ofsted.gov.uk/resources/admission-and-discharge-secure-accommodation

Sentencing Guidelines Council (SGC) (2009) *Overarching Principles – Sentencing Youths: Definitive Guideline*. London: SGC.

Solanki A and Utting D (2009) *Fine Art or Science Sentencers? Deciding between Community Penalties and Custody*. London: YJB.

UN (1990a) *Convention on the Rights of the Child*, Article 37(b).

UN (1990b) *Rules for the Protection of Juveniles Deprived of their Liberty*.

YJB (2012) *Monthly custody report*. Available at: www.justice.gov.uk/statistics/youth-justice/custody-data

YJB/MoJ (2012) *Youth Justice Statistics 2010/11, England and Wales*, January.

4
Desistance

Martin Stephenson

Introduction

This chapter critically examines how far the adoption of the closely allied 'what works' and risk-management approaches equips practitioners to contribute to the key outcome of preventing reoffending by young people. It argues that the current approaches, through the narrowness of the research methodology, the limited nature of findings and the overemphasis on risk management, constrain practitioners in understanding and participating effectively in enabling the processes of desistance.

The main theories underpinning desistance are explored and the potential mechanisms and circumstances that appear influential for young and older people stopping offending and sustaining their cessation are discussed. Finally, the implications of desistance studies for practitioners and the meaning of effectiveness are analysed.

Most of the discussion of desistance here relates to young people who have repeatedly offended and have been drawn well into the youth justice system as opposed to those whose offending behaviour is more short-lived.

Relationship between desistance and what works and risk-management approaches

It has been argued that the widespread adoption of the what works approach across criminal justice has, paradoxically, constrained effectiveness in reducing reoffending. Governments and their civil servants have been beguiled by the shiny certainties of an experimental approach akin to that used in medicine. Where the Cochrane Collaboration conducts systematic reviews using the gold standard of randomised control trials (RCTs), ultimately feeding into NICE (National Institute for Health and Care Excellence) guidance determining the effectiveness of different treatments in clinical and cost terms, so the Campbell Collaboration seeks to mirror this for criminal justice (Hough 2010: 13).

The concept of treatment has deep roots in criminal justice and has recently flourished as part of the evidence-based approach. From meta-analysis evidence, accredited programmes have been prescribed for adults in the criminal justice system, while for young people, a more flexible but similar doctrine has prevailed whereby systematic reviews commissioned by the Youth Justice Board (YJB) have been distilled into key elements of effective practice (KEEPs). From a practitioner's perspective, however, this approach has over-promised and under-delivered; the limitations of the nature and clarity of the evidence base have often been ignored. The findings of systematic reviews of programmes for reducing reoffending have been critically summarised thus:

▶ Insufficient high-quality research to provide many confident conclusions

▶ The body of 'what works' knowledge is incomplete and often inconsistent

▶ Some programmes sometimes produce positive results.

(Hough 2010: 13)

Now, while it is clearly valuable to be able to identify interventions that produce positive results, it is argued that there are fundamental flaws in this approach. One major issue is that of replicability. When they were first rolled out and evaluated, several programmes were shown to have a considerable impact on reoffending. However, when these initiatives went to scale, the effects disappeared. Proponents of the what works approach tend to state that implementation on a larger scale impairs programme integrity. However, this may simply conceal a significant problem (Stephenson *et al* 2011: 22–24). Whereas RCTs and quasi-experimental designs enable evaluation research to attribute cause confidently (ie they have high internal validity), they often have limited external validity (ie applicability to other circumstances). While there is a case to answer in terms of the theory and practice of implementation of scaled-up programmes, the weaker external validity may be due to the blind spots of the what works research approach: that is, it does not identify the mechanisms through which the positive effects are achieved. The 'how', the 'why' and the 'in what circumstances positive effects are achieved' are vital questions; the answers may explain the failure of replicability or why a given programme has a positive, negative or neutral effect on a particular individual.

What works has fitted neatly into the triangulation of politics, whereby the traditional divisions of right and left have been sidestepped in favour of a pragmatic 'what works is what matters' approach. Masquerading as a common-sense approach unencumbered by values, what works has combined simplicity of message with an ostensibly scientific method. Conceptually, it has nullified the complexities and ambiguities of the criminal justice system and the conflict between punishment and rehabilitation. The reliance on these valuable but necessarily narrow findings has stunted the development of middle-level theorising, which might afford greater insight into the mechanisms of change, potentially enabling greater replicability.

The overemphasis on RCTs and quasi-experimental research designs has crowded out more qualitative work, often necessary in understanding the individual and complex stories of personal change – in this instance, desistance from crime. While many of the studies are empirical, they lack the robustness of RCTs in attributing cause. However, they are vital for understanding the processes of desistance.

The practitioners and to some extent the participants have at times become viewed as constants – the dosage of a specific treatment is administered to achieve the desired effect – so much so that proponents have been accused of the 'zombification' of youth justice practitioners who now perform 'Korrectional Karaoke' (Pitts 2001). While such parodies are entertaining and ignore the desire for consistency in decision-making on grounds of equity and social justice, they underline the over-simplification that policymakers have been tempted into. The first chief executive of the YJB believed that KEEPs would enable practitioners to do 'exactly what it says on the tin'. If the mechanisms for desistance are at least partly related to the exercise of professional judgement, knowledge and skills, rather than rigid adherence to the application of whatever is in the tin, then effectiveness has been inadvertently reduced.

Rutter (2005: 2) poses four key questions about risk factor research: 'Is the association valid? If valid, does it represent a causal effect? If there is a causal influence, what element in the experience or circumstance provides the risk and by what mechanism does it operate? And does the risk operate in all the people in all circumstances or is it contingent on particular individual characteristics or a particular social context?' The current what works evidence base tends to answer questions one and two and then struggles with questions three and four.

The what works methodologies are usually closely entwined with the correctional paradigm for practice (McNeill 2004: 242). Ironically, while the what works evaluation framework produces mass effects without insight into the mechanisms whereby a practitioner can translate the findings readily into work with a young person, the risk management approach focuses almost exclusively on the likelihood of the individual young person reoffending. Crudely, actuarial instruments such as *Asset* are intended to provide the diagnosis through identifying salient risk factors, while the what works findings provide the treatment list. How far these two sets of evidence can be integrated readily by practitioners is open to question.

The deceptive certainties and comforting simplicities of the risk-management approach have drawn numerous challenges (Kemshall 2003; Smith 2006; Case and Haines 2009), but in the context of desistance studies and their implications for practice, there have been a number of other indirect and insidious influences: again the problem is that there is little emphasis on how risks operate to affect behaviour. The approach tends to ascribe all relevant causes of offending and responsibility to the individual and there have been numerous negative consequences. Little research has been carried out using the experiences of young people themselves and their reactions to interventions and why sometimes they work and sometimes they do not (Pitts 2003; Case 2006; Smith 2006). Risk factors are not neat constants and are often inherently more dynamic than actuarial assessment systems like *Asset* can cope with. It may be that the meaning of risk factors changes with use (Kemshall 2003) and are often specific to a particular context (Pitts 2003). In addition to downplaying the sociocultural context, there is relatively little emphasis on the personal agency of young people and the whole process remains largely uninformed by human rights. Inevitably, using a risk-dominated approach, the focus of the practitioner is on the perceived deficits of the young person and the potential areas of threat they may pose. Arguably, this neglects the whole area of psychological motivation and the evidence that concentrating on weaknesses and faults is less likely to facilitate positive personal change.

Allied to the what works approach, the risk-management discourse has been accused of overemphasising the use of tools and programmes at the expense of developing practitioners' knowledge and skills in facilitating the change process through their relationship with the young person (McNeill 2004). Knowledge of risk factors does not necessarily reveal motives for the actual committing of offences. Yet, as Sampson and Themelis (2009: 124) contend, it is knowledge about motives and reasons for offending that helps practitioners understand the decision-making processes of the young person, which in turn informs practitioners about how to work effectively with that particular young person.

Clearly it is beneficial for practitioners to be able to avail themselves of the findings of meta-analyses and to appreciate which programmes, on balance, appear to have positive effects (and avoid those that have negative effects). But knowledge of the general is often of little help to the particular. There is no finely graded series of treatments with detailed guidance on administering dosage. Indeed, Lipsey, the author of the most well known meta-analysis of 400 studies, warned: 'The inherent fuzziness of these coded categories makes futile any discussion of whether behaviour modification, or whatever your particular pet treatment might be, is universally superior to, say, family counselling' (Lipsey 1996: 74).

For practitioners grappling with the challenge of effectiveness, it is the omissions from the what works findings that are often more significant than their content. These findings cannot be routinely applied, given that, while some programmes work in some circumstances for some young people, they clearly do not for others. Again Lipsey (1996: 77) qualifies the meta-analysis findings: 'There is wide variation ranging from circumstances in which treatment actually seems to increase delinquency to those in which the reductions are quite substantial.'

It is all very well to give broad-brush advice that interventions should minimise risk factors and maximise protective factors but there is very little in the way of information and guidance on how and in what circumstances this should be done. By focusing on the mechanisms by which young people stop offending, desistance studies are perhaps more likely to provide some of the answers as to how practitioners can devise effective interventions for particular young people.

What is desistance?

Desistance is the process by which people come to cease and to sustain cessation of offending, with or without formal intervention.

(Weaver and McNeill 2008: 132)

This definition contains a number of interesting points about desistance relevant to the development of practice. Desistance is a process or a series of processes rather than a simple single event, with the implication that it occurs over time. It also carries the implication that is not necessarily straightforward and may be reversed on occasion. In contrast to research on the onset of crime, desistance studies examine the reasons for the absence rather than the presence of something. Desistance appears to be an active process rather than passive. As defined above, it is a two-stage process: stopping, and stopping permanently. This is often referred to as primary and secondary desistance respectively (Farrall and Calverley 2006: 2).

Given its more permanent nature, the process of secondary desistance is normally seen as more fundamental, often involving significant changes in the self-perception of the desister and a new approach to life. However, in working with adolescents, where arguably a week is a long time and periods of intervention are relatively brief, primary desistance may assume more significance. The fact that desistance often appears to occur without any clear link to formal intervention is telling. It reminds practitioners that effectiveness is not necessarily a reflection of the extent or nature of their intervention: the processes can be both complex and unpredictable.

Theories of offending and desistance

The overwhelming majority of theoretical work on crime deals with onset rather than cessation. Consequently, the focus is usually on prevention rather than desistance. Few theories present a complete explanation of the whole cycle from commencement to cessation. The explanation of desistance is often inferential rather than explicit. In any event, as with the onset of crime, desistance may well be multifactorial and practitioners may find that theories which can be readily integrated will form the basis for the development of their thinking on desistance.

Three broad theoretical models exist as a basis for practice development: maturation, social bonds, and narrative theory. Maturational change theories derive from the age–crime curve which, as an empirical finding, is robust but perhaps little understood. Social bonds theory offers a good link between the literature on desistance studies and mainstream literature on social control. This suggests that, for teenagers, the strength of social bonding – to education, training or employment (ETE) and to family – explains movements in and out of offending. Where social ties exist, they restrict opportunities to offend (as in full-time employment and higher levels of parental supervision) and their breaking contains the potential for loss. Conversely, their absence can create opportunities for crime and there is less to lose. Narrative theories, which often rely on qualitative research, emphasise the importance of subjective change. They examine changes in a person's self-identity through the creation of a new narrative of their lives and their increasing social inclusion. These 'redemption' scripts of desisters tend to be characterised by changing motivation, increased concern for others and planning for and having hope for the future (Maruna 2001).

Looking across these theories should enable practitioners to avoid focusing exclusively on cognitive changes in the young person and to work with other agencies to create legitimate opportunities and help the development of ties to, for example, education and family.

Models of desistance

	Individual	Structural	Integrationist
Key features	Sharp rise in offending in early teens with a peak in late teens/early adulthood, and a decrease thereafter. Age–crime curve. Age acts across social, temporal and economic conditions	Emphasises connection between desistance and external circumstances, which constitute turning points such as marriage, parental responsibility, employment	Emphasises subjective change and the creation of a new identity, which has little room for offending. The role of agency is important but so too are social circumstances
Causal mechanisms	Physical, mental and biological changes of maturation. Increase in legitimate opportunities and decrease in benefits from offending	Social and institutional ties create a stake in conformity to adult behavioural norms. Institutional ties act as informal social controls by reducing opportunities for offending and the motivation owing to disapproval and loss of status	A new narrative is created to support an identity with a higher level of motivation for conventional goals. Coupled with a greater concern for others and developing legitimate plans for the future, this leads to a rejection of offending
Weaknesses	Age in itself is not a singular explanation. It ignores the impact of social or institutional processes and does not readily explain desistance among teenagers	Ties are not simply exogenous forces. Their strength is partly determined by the decisions of the individual. This underplays the role of agency	Highly complex set of interactions and very difficult to perceive the sequencing between subjective and social change
Implications for practice	Encourage participation in activities that have pro-social recognition. Create legitimate opportunities seen to be of more benefit than offending	Focus on developing attachments to ETE and positive family relationships. Build on accessing and increasing social capital	Focus on developing strengths; minimise emphasis on negatives; engender hope for change; enhance planning and decision-making skills

Salient features of desistance

There are a number of social and personal factors and processes that studies have identified as being associated with desistance. The overriding issue is that desistance follows the life course, in that offending usually begins in the early teenage years, reaches a peak in late adolescence or young adulthood and withers away before 30 years of age. Several other factors associated with desistance also appear to be age-related, such as gaining employment and forming significant life partnerships. This obviously has important implications for practitioners working with young people in the youth justice system hoping to assimilate the findings of these studies. In the first instance, there may be little evidence of change in the earlier years; second, experiences that might be a turning point later in life, such as becoming a parent, could be far less positive if they take place during the teenage years. This of course places an emphasis on the judgement and ability of the practitioner to align their approach with the details and particular circumstances of a young person's life.

Gaining employment and forming stable significant life partnerships appear to be two powerful influences. However, the effects are age graded and to some extent appear to be dependent on quality: so, for example, a job is needed with a degree of security and sense of responsibility. Equally, studies have indicated that it is not marriage in itself that is important for desistance but rather the quality of the relationship and the offending experiences of the partner. Other influential processes include taking on parental responsibilities, the break up of delinquent peer groups and the impact of the criminal justice system, particularly repeated imprisonment. The nature of an individual's motivation to stop reoffending appears to be an element, while increasing feelings of shame about past behaviours has also been seen to be part of the desistance process. Combining several of these processes, so that the individual has in effect accomplished an identity shift, seems to be key for many people who desist.

The evidence base

The systematic investigation of desistance has only really gathered pace in criminology in recent years and inevitably there are major gaps in our knowledge. Much of the desistance literature is based on either longitudinal datasets (eg Sampson and Laub 1993) or one-off retrospective research (eg Graham and Bowling 1995). Several studies have followed the careers of adults once they enter the criminal justice system (eg LeBel *et al* 2008; Farrall 2002; Maruna 2001).

A significant amount of the longitudinal material is from outside the UK or from a period where the experience of adolescence was quite different (eg West and Farrington 1993). More recent UK-based longitudinal studies include the Edinburgh Study of Youth Transitions and Crime (eg Smith 2006; McAra and McVie 2010) and the Peterborough Adolescent and Younger Adult Development Study. The Sheffield Desistance Study is particularly useful on the deceleration of offending by young adults and combines longitudinal data with a focus on changing attitudes and values within the context of desistance (Shapland and Bottoms 2011).

Qualitative accounts by young people are particularly valuable in giving insight into how and why desistance occurs but there are very few studies involving teenagers and the sample sizes are usually small (Murray 2010, 2011; Haigh 2009; Sampson and Themelis 2009).

There is a dearth of information regarding gender and ethnicity and desistance. One of the few studies to have considered female desistance found that the processes for females appeared to be different from those of males, in that becoming an adult as marked by the usual transitions of leaving home, finishing school and becoming a parent applied to them but not to their male counterparts (Graham and Bowling 1995). Another study found that desistance for young men involved more practical reasons such as employment whereas for young women relational issues such as caring for others were more important (Barry 2006).

Only relatively recently have desistance studies started to examine the implications for policy and practice, and these have largely focused on adults subject to probation (McNeill 2004). Very few studies have looked at what qualitative desistance research means for work with young people (Haigh 2009; Sampson and Themelis 2009; Murray 2010, 2011).

Figure 4.1: The age–crime curve

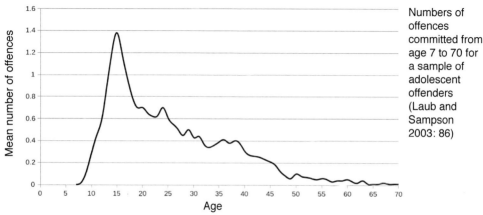

Most of the evidence indicates that even those individuals who get most involved in crime tend to reduce offending as they get older. As the graph above highlights, there is a marked deceleration between the ages of 20 and 30 with an eventual complete cessation of offending for many. While this provides some comfort to practitioners, in that there is always hope, there is no avoiding the fact that intervention is required often at the time of peak offending. Given the shape of this curve it is arguably very important for youth justice practitioners to understand the maturational processes that appear to be associated with desistance in order to foster their development in young people during their adolescence.

Sampson and Laub (1993) put forward the notion of age-graded social control based on the strength of the bond between an individual and society. When an individual's bond to society becomes attenuated, crime is more likely to occur. The nature of these ties and the informal social constraints they create vary as individuals age. So sequentially, over the life course, parenting styles and emotional attachment to parents in childhood are superseded by school attachment and peers in adolescence and by marital stability and employment in adulthood. Thus institutions such as marriage, parenthood and employment, through the relationships they engender, help create social bonds that in turn bring about informal social control. Long-standing relationships could lead to the accumulation of resources and an increasing stake in conformity. In this context, desistance is the result of a potentially protracted process. It could also occur indirectly or by default as relationships, for example with employment, are not formed initially to stop offending – desistance comes as a by-product.

In their initial studies, Sampson and Laub put great emphasis on the structural notion of turning points but later modified this by placing more stress on human agency and choice (Sampson and Laub 2005). This is consistent with more recent work such as that by Maruna, whose main focus has been on the subjective, internal changes related to desistance whereby desisters recast their identities, developing a vision of their futures as pro-social and achievable (Maruna 2001). In contrast to the redemption scripts of the desisters, those who continue to offend are guided by a 'doom-laden' script, with little sense that they may be able to change their fate. How far young people have written their scripts or created any firm sense of identity is very much open to question when compared to these adult narratives.

Developing the concept of the accumulation and expenditure of capital, Barry (2006) argues that both offending and desistance can be seen as part of young people's success or failure in negotiating the key transitions to adulthood. For many young people, the barriers to acquiring legitimate capital are such that it may be easier to acquire capital in terms of status and respect in their peer group by offending.

Processes of desistance

The main theoretical approaches in outline reveal relatively little that is of practical use to a practitioner, although their implications in terms of active involvement and the potential to influence outcomes are very different. Models of desistance that are more deterministic and dependent on structure or age imply a less influential role, while those with an emphasis on agency may be more amenable to influence by a practitioner. To the extent that most if not all behaviour is learned, offending behaviour can potentially be unlearned and new patterns of behaviour acquired. In order to draw out some of the implications for practice, it is necessary to examine the processes that are ostensibly involved in desistance.

Turning points

In contrast to the onset of offending, which can be characterised by drift, desistance often appears to be a more active process in the sense of a commitment to refrain from offending. The concept of a 'turning point', defined as an alteration or deflection in a long-term pathway or trajectory, is seen as crucial to the process of desistance (Sampson and Laub 2005). These points are usually seen as key life events often connected with the transition to adulthood rather than epiphanies. They are institutional or structural events such as marriage or employment. They involve to a varying extent new opportunities that 'knife off' the past, provide circumstances where there is increased supervision and monitoring, and opportunities for more social support and growth. These new contexts afford the opportunity for a revision or transformation of identity. One immediate challenge is to identify potential comparable turning points in adolescence, which may for example be re-engagement with mainstream education or a change in accommodation and care circumstances. However, a critical issue is the relationship between these turning points and human agency: purposeful choice and individual will. Reconciling the exercise of choice in the concept of a structural turning point is an increasing preoccupation of desistance studies. As Abbott (1997: 102) describes it: 'A major turning point has the potential to open a system the way a key has the potential to open a lock … *action* is necessary to complete the turning' (italics mine).

One explanatory framework for examining the processes of desistance integrates the three phases of offending – onset, maintenance and desistance – with the three phases of youth transitions – childhood, youth and adulthood (Barry 2006). One advantage of this approach is that it connects offending and desistance as two aspects of the same change process rather than desistance simply being the absence of the original problems. Using Bourdieu's theory of capital, Barry argues that, while the failure to accrue legitimate capital can lead to offending to replace this, the acquisition and expenditure of legitimate capital is central to the desistance process through successful transitions.

Social capital is all about the valued relations with significant others. For young people, family, school and peer groups are the main potential sources of social capital. Economic capital by contrast represents harder resources such as income and assets. Cultural capital derives from education and art in particular and includes those qualifications and competencies that comprise an individual's cultural entity. Finally, symbolic capital is seen as the encompassing resource derived from the other three forms of capital.

If transitions to adulthood involve the acquisition of these forms of capital, it can be seen how offending could fill the gap if capital is not successfully acquired through more legitimate means. Young people with challenging home backgrounds or experiencing care instability through being looked after and those detached from school clearly lack the network of resources available to others and might find it in delinquent peer groups. Clearly, young people from financially disadvantaged backgrounds might find crime to be their main source of economic capital. Gaining a street reputation through offending could provide the main source for acquiring symbolic capital.

Capital gained during adolescence through illegitimate means tends not to be enduring and of itself can impede successful transitions. So, while offending during childhood and youth can offer opportunities for acquiring capital, given the paucity of other opportunities for gaining legitimate social recognition, its value weakens over time. Once employment, marriage and parenthood become available options, not only do people have more opportunities for gaining social recognition but the social costs of continued offending reduce its value.

Thus the age–crime curve charts how the sources of capital shift in both quality and quantity as people get older and other commitments come to the fore. The answer to how capital in its differing forms can reduce offending may lie in the expenditure of capital through giving to others. The two principal ways this occurs is through taking on responsibilities such as a job or family, or wanting to make good and contribute to the community. These are continually emphasised in narratives of desistance and perceived as important parts of a person's new identity. In this model, offending and desistance are not as associated with age *per se* as with levels of enduring, legitimate responsibility.

Transitions loom large for those working in youth justice as so many of the young people are facing dislocated or premature transitions. Detachment from education and training is commonplace, delaying or restricting entry to the labour market. Leaving home early and independent living affects a higher proportion of these young people than their peers. And custody significantly disrupts all aspects of transition, arguably including the development of essential skills of planning for the future and assuming individual responsibility.

Desisting from offending is clearly closely connected to a successful transition to adulthood, although some researchers have gone further and argued that desistance from crime is actually part of a package of role behaviours that define adulthood (Massoglia and Uggen 2010). This idea accords with the notion that delinquency and antisocial behaviour are relatively normal features of adolescence and that offending declines with age and maturity.

Transitions though are not simply about the acquisition of material independence but also very much about the assumption of certain roles and the recognition of this by others. Age colours our judgement of the acceptability of certain behaviours. For instance, binge drinking among children is seen as both illegal and age-inappropriate; it is illegal but is considered more age-appropriate for 17 year olds; and it is legal but is considered age-inappropriate for those over 40.

Other features characterising recent generations is that youth is being significantly extended, with traditional markers of adulthood achieved much later, such as staying on at school longer and delayed entry to the labour market. This perhaps explains the persistence of traditionally teenage behaviours through some people's twenties, particularly young men (Graham and Bowling 1995). The extension of the youth and criminal justice systems may be both the cause and effect of this. Contact with the criminal justice system, particularly through imprisonment, attenuates this transition to adult status as it tends to reduce inmates to a weaker, more dependent role while disrupting ties to employment and family.

One longitudinal survey supported by in-depth interviews in the USA tested the association between desistance and adult status (Massoglia and Uggen 2010). The researchers found that the reciprocal relationship between desistance and other transitions was central in understanding progress towards adult status. Their conclusions, consistent with the social bonds theory, were that conventional adult role behaviour gradually fostered desistance, through increasing commitment and consequent discouraging of behaviours that could jeopardise the role. For practitioners working with teenagers, ironically, this finding underlines the fact that for many adolescents the very attraction of delinquency is that aspects of it ape adult behaviour. Yet, for those in their late twenties, such behaviour would seem to reduce their feelings of adult status. In this context, it is interesting to note just how important the need to be treated and recognised as an adult by those in authority is to many young people in the youth justice system.

Increasingly, desistance studies have come to view progression from offending to abstinence as produced by a complex interaction between internal and external factors. The internal factors include levels of motivation, willingness to change and perhaps the exercise of 'active resilience' (Murray 2010). The influence of agency has been given more prominence recently, but its relationship to social and environmental factors and the part it plays in turning points remains underdeveloped. From a practitioner's standpoint, the dichotomy between internal and external factors could be a useful conceptual tool but there is little in the literature that helps to disentangle the role of internal or subjective change from social and environmental change. Clearly, such changes are likely to have reciprocal effects that may be reinforcing: a young person may decide to re-engage with education and choose a particular course and through attending college and succeeding academically or vocationally may increase ambition and motivation still further. The relative balance of subjective and social change in the sequencing of events – for example, does attitudinal change precede crucial new attachments such as employment, marriage and starting a family? – is important knowledge for practitioners.

One study specifically examined this interrelationship, albeit using the experience of imprisoned adults, and found that personal identity, self-narratives and positive mindset had a measurable effect on outcomes (LeBel et al 2008). This echoed the cognitive themes identified in the redemption scripts of desistance compared to the 'condemnation' scripts of persisters (Maruna 2001). Hope, in the sense of an individual's belief in their self-efficacy, appeared to enable a person to choose and take advantage of positive social opportunities.

There are few studies that look specifically at the experiences of young people who desist but those that do indicate that desistance is not a passive process. The fact that desistance studies, in contrast to studies of offending, examine actions that are not performed perhaps almost by definition underestimates just how active a process desistance, at least in the maintenance phase, has to be (Murray 2011). Given that, unlike adults' antisocial behaviour, offending may be much closer to the norm among young people, it may be that desistance is more challenging for them. Whatever the relative level of difficulty compared to adults, the twin processes of getting involved in crime and refraining from it could be characterised as 'drift in – struggle out'.

Inevitably, the transition from involvement in offending to not offending is complex. Even when the perceived cost of involvement in offending outweighs its benefits, moving away is not an easy or straightforward process (Haigh 2009). While adult desisters usually appear to have experienced a period of re-evaluation before deciding to desist, with the creation of a coherent narrative about their cessation (Maruna 2001), it may not be as dramatic for young people (Murray 2011). This may be simply because their experience in offending is briefer or because issues of identity are at a more malleable stage. Nevertheless they do experience shifts in their interpretation of their circumstances, which are part of a process making it possible for change to occur (Haigh 2009). This reinterpretation process stresses the importance of choice and decision-making, particularly as the shift away from involvement in crime can be gradual and include reversals.

The narratives of young people chart how hard they have to work to disrupt their existing routines and habitual thinking when offending is an integral part of their lives. Current automatic actions have to become doubted so that alternative choices can be considered. How a young person comes to challenge their existing way of life and to engage with alternative ways of thinking and acting takes place in their particular social and environmental circumstances but involves the exercise of their agency. The term 'active resilience' has been coined to describe how young people resist offending and captures the young person's own choices and will in building their capacity to cope without offending (Murray 2010).

It may be unlikely that desistance generally occurs through dramatic, short-term change but 'is a gradual process of small decisions, small behavioural or lifestyle changes and consequent readjustment to one's self- and group identity' (Shapland and Bottoms 2011: 264). One of the interesting findings from the Sheffield Desistance Study is that most of the young adults who offended persistently nevertheless felt shame about their behaviour and shared conventional social values. While it must be borne in mind that this evidence is derived from young adults who have probably undergone important processes of social maturation, the findings may have important lessons for practitioners who work with adolescents. If conventional goals and values are commonplace among young adults who offend persistently then this begs the question of why they continue to offend. Clearly there is a tension between these values and the young adults' intention not to offend on the one hand, and their social networks and circumstances on the other. This underlines two important points: that much offending is related to specific contexts and situations; and that wanting to desist is a necessary but not sufficient condition for actual desistance – there is a big gap between 'wish' and 'deed'. Now it may well be that many adolescents involved in persistent offending have more of a commitment to delinquent norms than young adults do; but if that is not the case then the emphasis for practitioners needs to be on assisting a young person to avoid certain circumstances and to move towards their underlying aspirations, which may well be fairly conventional. As the evidence drawn from young people on summer arts colleges below indicates, this may require some significant changes in their routine daily activities and in their friendship networks.

Testimonies of young people attending summer arts colleges

Examination of the experiences of young people who have attended summer arts colleges (SACs) and successfully desisted provides some insight into how and why this occurred for these participants in what is a large-scale programme familiar to many practitioners in youth justice (Tarling and Adams 2012). Given that the young people had generally not been involved in full-time employment, the three main areas where they had ties and networks were school/college, peers and family. However, they were often detached from education, both physically in the sense that they were permanently excluded or long-term non-attenders, and socially in that they had formed relatively few attachments to friends and teachers while they were there. Family relationships were often marked by conflict caused at least in part by detachment from education and their peer networks tended to be delinquent or at least deemed to be a bad influence.

The point of departure for many of the young people seemed to be one of drift, characterised by fairly chaotic lifestyles, lacking in routine and almost nocturnal in some cases.

Nothing, I was literally doing nothing.

Andy

Like going out and drinking every day like, like doing nothing with my time, like waking up at 2 or 3 o'clock in the afternoon, doing nothing at all.

Eric

Despite enjoying some advantages that this lifestyle could bring, Eric also acknowledged its negativity:

Well, the best thing was like going out and getting leathered with my mates and that, but that was kind of the worst time as well, if you know what I mean?

Eric

An important effect of the programme was the replacement of the previously chaotic lifestyle by a series of relatively intense routines and activities. Given that the only externally imposed routines had been through school or college and more recently youth justice, the experience of positive routines in providing much-needed structure may be disproportionately important to adolescents.

Something to do, like a scheduled thing to do every day, so you're not just sitting around doing nothing.

Ian

Yes, it was a stepping stone of getting me out of that routine. I think if I didn't go then I probably would have still been the same. I probably wouldn't even think about getting back to college, I was happy in my life as it was and it wasn't good, to be honest.

Gary

Yeah, that helped me, because obviously as soon as I'd finished the summer arts college, a couple of weeks later I'd started college, so I was already in the routine of getting up, going to college and coming back, so it helped a lot.

Andy

Their removal from a delinquent peer network was most often cited as the primary reason for cessation of offending during the summer. They highlighted that they were disassociated from their offending peers during the summer period when many of them felt particularly at risk.

Yes. It helped me stay away from the wrong people that I was hanging around with, because obviously I wasn't using my summer to be with them, because I was on tag in the summer holidays anyway, so I only had like, from the time it started, I only had a couple of hours left before I had to be inside anyway. It didn't give me the chance to hang around with them people, so they kind of just moved on and forgot about me, which was good.

Brian

Actually, it did help keep me out of trouble ... cos I knew that if I was in there at certain times, I wouldn't mix with the people I meet. It was good that I was there. A few of them did [get picked up by the police] while I was there, so it was good.

Damion

I wasn't looking to stop hanging around with them, well, obviously I stopped getting in trouble, so it made me realise that I wasn't hanging round with them so much, obviously they weren't doing a great deal for me.

Brian

Because you're not like out in the streets all day, you're doing something like with yourself. Like I thought it was all right there, I thought it was quite good. It kept me doing something, it kept me occupied every day. So, rather than being out on the streets, drinking or smoking and stuff like that ... When I was doing the summer college it was keeping busy.

Claire

While diversion from delinquent peer groups and containment were identified as the reason they kept out of trouble during the programme, the unaccustomed intensity also seems to have played a part:

No, because every time I used to go I used to get shattered and I used to go to sleep early.

Jo

Practicalities also played an important part in ensuring that young people continued to attend:

> *Yes, obviously we always had, well, we had a lift there and we had a lift back, which helped out a lot, actually, because, you know, if we didn't have a lift, I don't reckon half of us would have come, because it's getting out of bed in the six weeks holidays, you know.*
>
> Andy

> *Yes, because they woke me up, otherwise if I weren't going to get picked up or nothing, I wouldn't have ended up going.*
>
> Jo

Clearly removal from their offending peer group and filling up their daytime may have only had a temporary diversionary effect and it was interesting to explore to what extent participation in the SAC programme acted as a trigger for more enduring change or reinforced decisions that had already been made to change.

One of the main objectives of the scheme was to re-engage these young people with mainstream education; comparing pre-and post-programme attendance and attitudes, this was achieved for a significant number of them. A series of ties were created which attached young people to the SAC and the learning experiences in it. This equipped them with the knowledge and confidence to extend these ties subsequently to school and college. Relationships with adults, both positive and negative, played an influential part in detachment from and reattachment to formal learning. During the programme the nature of the relationship with the artists was contrasted favourably with teachers in school. Two key aspects that were highlighted were respectful treatment, as if they were equal adults, and the use of humour:

> *They was all nice and everything, but it's like they treated us more like adults than we was like criminals or like kids.*
>
> Kate

> *Just the respect on it, really, they're more respectful to you.*
>
> Harry

Yeah, basically most of the time we're treated like young kids, but we're not, that's what makes that so bad, because since a young age I've never been taken as a child, like I don't want no one to take me for a mug, because I grew up to be a man from a young age, yeah, so I don't want someone to talk to me like a kid, so most people, when you treat them like adults, they turn out to be like adults.

James

Another area of change that endured beyond the SAC programme appears to have been in relationships with their families.

Oh, she's got a lot better opinion of me now. I know she can't exactly have a bad opinion of me, well, she can if she wants. Like I say she was distraught at the time, but now, we never fall out or anything, but she's just got like a higher opinion of me, because I'm actually doing something now. Like I used to get my money off her, at the time, so it was like wake up, get money off her and do whatever. Now I don't take money off her or anything.

Gary

Because like I know for a fact, if I was at home all day, I'd be waking up late, I'd have nothing to do but cause trouble and create mayhem for my sisters and my mum and stuff and there'd be just all arguments, fire blazing all the time, so it just kept me busy, it kept me on my feet, so kept me up and running.

Damion

In [the past] she was 'you are wasting the electric' and me screaming 'shut up' and just stupid things like that, but when I went to the summer college, I was able to go 'I have some photos here, look at these'. Like there was one point where we wouldn't ever talk really and that, but now if I have the slightest problem ... then we sit down and have a good proper chin wag and that, we have got a bond now.

Kate

One slightly surprising area that produced positive social bonds for many of the young people was the relationship between those attending the programme. Many of the young people retained warm and positive memories of their fellow group members and some forged enduring new friendships:

It was more like a funny family than anything else, funny when we were there, we had jokes.

Damion

We all got to be like one big family, so they were all big brothers to me, except X who was like a little one. Like we were all like proper close, I don't know, I just enjoyed being around them all, I really miss them now. I want to go back, I want to see them all again, I miss all of them.

Kate

The iatrogenic (unintentionally adverse) effects of the SACs appeared to be more limited than in other programmes. The formation of the group seems to have been construed very positively, with many participants deriving comfort from the fact that they were all in it together, with the arts being a new experience, having no history of failure for them. Their shared experience in the demanding routines of the SAC appears to have fostered positive social bonds between group members rather than competitive, risky behaviours. This is not to ignore the fact that for some young people the composition of the group may have led to increased conflict and possibly indirectly or directly to subsequent offending or at least being breached.

The intensity of the whole process seems to have been sufficient to create a turning point in some young people's lives and enabled many of them to weave a stronger narrative about their lives. It could be seen as reflecting a broader trend that has been observed across behavioural and social sciences, which stresses that behavioural change is more easily achieved when people work towards positive approach goals rather than negative avoidance goals.

But if summer arts colleges provided a new context for the elaboration of positive routines and productive relationships with both adults and peers, what part did internal or subjective factors play in bringing about sustained behavioural change? Certainly the young people's testimonies indicate that the SACs enabled some of them to change their view of themselves.

… it was good, the summer arts thing gave me a lot of confidence actually … A lot of confidence and it gave me the strength to actually leave them … [delinquent peers]. Because I had low self-esteem, I had no confidence, no nothing when I went there, then when I'd finished, I was like a better person, I had so much confidence

... People was telling me that I was doing good things, instead of me hearing bad things all the time.

Kate

Obviously it's independence in myself and belief that I can do things, not that I can't do things and not that I've got to hang around with a crowd and I've got to fit in with them ... You know, I'm my own person, I am who I am.

Andy

It changed my view of how I was as a person.

Caitlin

For others, the decision to change appeared to have already been made. Sometimes this may have been the effect of custody or an Intensive Supervision and Surveillance Programme (ISSP) or the reactions of parents:

ISSP has changed me too, it is like all them nights when I am sat in on my own having to think about what I have got to do with myself and where I need to pick myself up and what I need to do to change, like it actually kicked in, cos I was just sat there and I thought, right I can not go around battering people or like causing arguments, I need to grow up, I have left school so now I need to get a job, I can't be that person any more, I just need to sort myself out.

Damion

Well, when I was in there [custody], you don't have much to do except think. When I was in there and I was thinking every day like that I was going to change and that when I got out and like I did, because the art helps and all.

Dominic

Yeah, definitely, like when I got done for this offence I did, like my family were distraught, like my mum was and everything, I just didn't like myself or nothing, I just wanted to change, I realised like I needed to get something done with my time, do you know what I mean, something constructive.

Gary

I didn't think it was as bad, it wasn't like it was a huge robbery, it was little. I personally thought at the time that my robbery was a little robbery, but then the amount of times I've heard like about my robbery, it sounds bigger and bigger every time, but I didn't think the woman that I robbed would be so like affected by it. Like that was then, now I know how she feels and I'm really sorry, but then I didn't really think she'd be that affected, I just thought it would be a quick thing, a bit of fun.

Brian

However, while the decision to change appeared to be a prerequisite for desistance, it did not in general appear to be sufficient. Many young people felt they needed the new opportunities afforded by the SAC programme, reinforced by the support of peers and the motivation of key staff, to help them translate thought into action. Some seemed aware of the interplay between the structural and subjective elements and that it was the package that helped constitute a turning point for them.

Yeah, it were all combined, basically it did help me change. To change you can't say right I want to change and then not do anything about it, but like the motivation and the whole things combining together and stuff, that like helped me, like summer arts college helped me to change, but I didn't go to summer arts college and think right, I want to change now.

Karl

I think my circumstances have changed the way I approached it, I don't think I've changed.

Brian

Exemplifying the narrative approach to creating a new positive identity, as well as recognising turning points in his life, was the young person who kept photographs of key events in his life:

I keep all the pictures of pivotal moments in my life, I don't take a lot of pictures, I'm talking about my driving licence, my first passport, that's [his SAC photograph] one of the pictures in the long array of me growing up, that's like the delinquency phase as I call it.

Leon

Commenting some three and a half years after his SAC experience, this young man (now undertaking a degree at university) had always kept the picture of his artwork on display wherever he had lived to remind himself 'where I've come from and where I'm going'.

Echoing the findings that a redemption script includes developing more of a sense of community and a desire to contribute or pay back, one young person was keen to run his:

> *... own programme based on the summer college that I went to in X because there is nothing there for kids, so I wanted to run something similar to that. Basically there is nothing to do, cos like on my estate I can see kids getting into trouble and breaking windows because they haven't got anything to do, so, I thought that this would help them too.*

> Damion

One major criticism of the what works approach that may be relevant in understanding the relative success of the SAC programme is that it can be very negative, concentrating on eliminating deficits and changing destructive and unwanted behaviours. By contrast, SACs, owing to their arts component and educational emphasis, possess more of a strengths-based approach. The emphasis is continuously on achievement and acquiring new skills in the context of forming a new, positive group culminating in professional and parental acclaim.

Part of the answer may also lie in just how positively young people viewed their learning at a SAC. They strongly rejected their negative experience of traditional education and contrasted their learning at the SAC very favourably. Perhaps for the first time learning was fun. Traditional education to them had been marked by boredom, conflict and an indelible sense of failure. The very nature of arts activities, which arguably removed the potential to fail, the use of embedded literacy and numeracy and the contractual nature of the learning that evolved all seemed to combine to evoke a powerful positive response.

In trying to understand the effects of this programme, one potentially enlightening theory is that of identity, enabling people to create a positive narrative that can recast an identity previously moulded by educational failure and characterised by offending. Perhaps SACs offer some individuals the opportunity and positive pressures to recast themselves with a different, much more positive storyline. Membership of the youth justice system is a badge of failure but membership of the SAC group is a hallmark of success. The project itself tends to assist this process of redefinition by identifying the young people as 'students', setting them a series of group and individual tasks that are demanding but achievable and fun, and crucially completing this process with public recognition of their new status through a nationally recognised qualification, the Arts Award, and a celebration event attended by parents/carers and local dignitaries.

Implications for practice

So what are the implications of this review of desistance studies for practice? The research into the mechanisms of desistance for young people is thin, partly because, for some, cessation of offending does not occur until later in life. However the paucity of the evidence may also be partly a reflection of the current overemphasis on the effectiveness of programmes. Studies of the processes underlying desistance move the knowledge and skills of the practitioner to centre stage. If achieving behavioural change is essentially a human process then the quality of the relevant relationships may be an important determinant of the outcomes. If this holds true, the personal qualities and skills of the practitioner as an agent of change assume much greater significance. Effectiveness in this context is as much about influencing relationships and processes positively as it is about introducing young people to particular programmes (McNeill 2004). In fact some of the evidence indicates that young people place more value on a supportive relationship with a non-judgemental adult who assists them to navigate their way through challenging circumstances rather than on a particular programme (France and Homel 2006).

If the real question is how we change the behaviour of a particular young person rather than simply know which interventions on balance have a positive effect on large groups, then different lessons are drawn from the desistance evidence base. These lessons, although often derived from the experience of adults, include:

◗ Working to support the efforts of the young person to cease offending

◗ Respecting and reinforcing their capacity to exert control over their lives

◗ Legitimate and respectful relationships despite their involuntary nature

◗ Focusing on human capital (the young person's motivation and capacity) and on increasing their social capital (gaining access to education and housing, for example).

Drawing on Hough (2010), a conceptual framework for practitioner effectiveness could include the following often interrelated elements to shape the response to and outcomes for young people who offend:

▶ Particular programmes or interventions the young person is exposed to

▶ Ethos of the team

▶ Personal qualities, skills and knowledge in the team

▶ Quality of leadership and morale in the team

▶ Responsiveness and resource levels of other agencies such as schools and housing

▶ Social economic context of the young person's neighbourhood

▶ Funding levels and resources including available programmes in the team

▶ Characteristics of the particular young person.

Even if particular interventions are available (and they are often not), while it is reasonable to expect some impact on the behaviour of some young people, clearly there are many other influences that could prove far more significant in affecting desistance. One way of moving beyond the relatively narrow conception of effective practice is to consider the craft of working with young people who offend (Hough 2010: 18). In a similar fashion to other practitioners such as teachers, youth justice practitioners need to deploy a set of craft skills at different levels. These can be divided into three broad groups of skills: social interaction, social advocacy, and casework style. The successful deployment of these skills has to be within the context of effective engagement here defined as: 'the positive participation and progression of a young person within a youth justice intervention' (Stephenson *et al* 2011: 72-96).

Social interaction skills include techniques for asserting authority and also for developing a positive relationship. They would cover, for example, the use of body language, communication skills and the ability to project empathy. Casework style would encompass the ability to match the young person to a particular activity or intervention, using techniques such as motivational interviewing and pro-social modelling, and using judgement to decide on the sequence of activities and actions given the multiple nature of challenges in many young people's lives. While these two skill sets are very much focused on enabling change to occur in an individual, the social advocacy skills of the practitioner need to be aimed outwards, in particular at other agencies, securing access to services and opportunities. Arguably, these skills need to be exercised more broadly in relation to welfare needs and particularly educational inclusion rather than simply criminogenic needs (McAra and McVie 2010: 200).

One set of skills and knowledge that could be used in gaining access for young people to education, health, housing and leisure services is social advocacy. Clearly, the youth justice practitioner has the court for a client and cannot simply be an offline advocate focusing solely on the young person's wishes. Despite this qualification, and acknowledging the potential tension between the two roles, the ability to speak on behalf of the young person and ensure that they are actively listened to and involved in decision-making by other agencies and services can be of critical importance. While part of this role is about ensuring their rights to participation, it is also very much about brokerage – that is, securing access to services that are not under the direct control of the youth offending service.

There is some evidence for the effectiveness of advocacy with looked after children and young people (Oliver, Knight and Candappa 2006). Given that many young people in the youth justice system have experienced being looked after, and that they generally share similar features of social exclusion in their lives, the findings of this study are a useful guide. The issues of concern to the young people surveyed included: maintaining contact with family and friends; problems with housing, welfare benefits and other entitlements; access to education services; legal problems, including immigration and custody of children; and health-related issues. All of these are relevant to young people in the youth justice system.

Not surprisingly perhaps, a survey of advocates identified a range of perceived practical and psychological benefits for the children and young people. This practitioner view was supported by the majority of children and young people, who reported high satisfaction with a range of important emotional and practical outcomes (Oliver, Knight and Candappa 2006: 10).

Despite the significant qualitative evidence of the benefits of advocacy to children and young people, the long-term cost-effectiveness of advocacy as a service is not yet supported by robust evidence (Brady 2011). Young people in the youth justice system do not usually have a statutory entitlement to an independent advocate except when they are looked after, care leavers or in custody in a secure training centre (STC). However, in these and other circumstances, there may be occasions when the youth justice practitioner enlists the aid of an advocate for a young person. In any event, exercising the skills and role of an advocate on behalf of young people would appear to be essential in enabling them to access legitimate opportunities for their development and promoting the creation of ties that could aid the process of desistance.

In relation to social advocacy, two areas are highlighted by empirical studies: practitioners need to take account of educational inclusion and working with parents. In the Edinburgh Study of Youth Transitions and Crime, early desistance from offending was associated with bonds with teachers and parents (Smith 2006: 13). The strength of the bonds with parents comprised the degree of parental monitoring and level of conflict with their children. There was a further interesting link in that the level of parents' commitment to school (but not that of the young person) was associated statistically with desistance from offending. These crossover ties between home and school are very important, providing 'bridging social capital'. Given the evidence from the SAC initiative, which has involved a wide sample of youth offending teams (YOTs) and indicates a patchy approach to working with parents/carers, this may be an important area for practice development.

While the relationship between attachment or rather detachment from school and offending has been explored in detail in recent years (Stephenson 2007) and the effects of underachievement and poor relationships in schools examined, one longitudinal study found that positive school and career orientation was associated with inhibiting the development of delinquent behaviour (Skorikov and Vondracek 2007). The researchers argue that vocational intentions and aspirations develop early and have a positive effect on the subsequent development of adolescent identity in other areas, seen as an important protective factor from offending. Again, experience from SACs indicates that familiarity among caseworkers with, for example, the further education system can often be limited. This seriously constrains their ability to act as advocates in this crucial area of opening up educational access and supporting young people's participation successfully.

The twin key objectives of the youth justice craft then are to develop human capital – a young person's skills, capacities and personal resilience – and social capital – extending the access of the young person and promoting their engagement in wider social networks and institutions, in particular schools and colleges but also cultural activities including leisure and sport.

In the exercise of this craft, language is crucially important. This is not simply taking account of any speech, language and communication difficulties that a young person might have, important though that is, but involves two other significant aspects. It has been argued that the very language of the dominant risk discourse leads practitioners to emphasise deficits and problems, which lie behind a risk-focused intervention, rather than the purpose and aspiration of the desistance-focused approach (McNeill 2004). Recent examination of the concepts of resilience and desistance, which are seen to be closely allied (Fitzpatrick 2011; Murray 2010, 2011), have highlighted that both concepts emphasise the capacity of individuals to overcome adversity and fit strengths-based and solution-focused practice. While it is essential to be alert to risks to the safety and welfare of the young person and to others, great care must be taken in not being led by the language into concentrating only on problems, deficits and vulnerability. Language matters at another level too. One of the memorable themes that emerges from several of the main desistance studies is that desisters are successful at creating a redemption narrative that sustains their self-belief, sometimes almost irrespective of the evidence. Current risk-dominated language could act to entrench the wrong kind of identity for a young person as an offender and reinforce any labelling processes, thereby inhibiting desistance (McNeill 2004; McAra and McVie 2010: 200).

Conclusions

Desistance studies, particularly where young people are concerned, are relatively underdeveloped but they indicate that the role of the practitioner in exercising their skills and judgement is arguably much more central to the process of reducing reoffending than with a risk-management model.

Far from simply applying the contents of the tin, an effective practitioner needs to be able to assimilate the limited available evidence, drawing on appropriate theoretical models, and to use these to refine their craft skills in becoming an 'empirical practitioner' (Trotter 1999). It is clear from the what works literature that one size does not and never will fit all. At best we have indications that certain interventions may achieve positive outcomes for some young people some of the time. The focus on what works research and the particular nature of the evidence and methodologies used have occluded insight into how and why and in what circumstances positive outcomes are achieved.

The answers to these questions may lie in the complex interplay between agency and structure for an individual young person and also the nature of their relationship with the different professionals involved in their life. The messages from desistance studies pose uncomfortable questions about effectiveness. If it is a process or series of processes that may take several years to ensure cessation, how is effectiveness to be judged in the short-term involvement of the youth justice practitioner? If the wider context of a young person's life, such as the lack of available educational provision, should prove intractable to the best efforts of the practitioner, how is effectiveness to be judged? Despite this, emerging evidence on desistance offers some salutary opportunities for the development of practitioners' skills and knowledge. Developing the necessary craft skills of social interaction, appropriate casework style and effective social advocacy can all be shaped positively through taking account of the growing body of evidence on desistance.

References

Abbott A (1997) 'On the concept of turning point', *Comparative Social Research*, 16: 85–105.

Barry M (2006) *Youth Offending in Transition: The Search for Social Recognition*. Abingdon: Routledge.

Brady L (2011) *Where Is My Advocate? A Scoping Report on Advocacy Services for Children and Young People in England*. London: Office of the Children's Commissioner (OCC).

Case S (2006) 'Young people at risk of what? Challenging risk-focused early intervention as crime prevention', *Youth Justice*, 6: 171–179.

Case S and Haines KR (2009) *Understanding Youth Offending: Risk Factor Research, Policy and Practice*. Cullompton: Willan.

Farrall S (2002) *Rethinking What Works With Offenders*. Cullompton: Willan.

Farrall S and Calverley A (2006) *Understanding Desistance from Crime*. Maidenhead: Open University Press (OUP).

Fitzpatrick C (2011) 'What is the difference between 'desistance' and 'resilience'? Exploring the relationship between two key concepts', *Youth Justice*, 11(3): 221–234.

France A and Homel A (2006) 'Societal access routes and developmental pathways: putting social structure and young people's voice into the analysis of pathways into and out of crime', *Australian and New Zealand Journal of Criminology*, 39(3): 295–309.

Graham J and Bowling B (1995) *Young People and Crime*. London: HMSO.

Haigh Y (2009) 'Desistance from crime: reflections on the transitional experiences of young people with a history of offending', *Journal of Youth Studies*, 12(3): 307–322.

Hough M (2010) 'Gold standard or fool's gold? The pursuit of certainty in experimental criminology', *Criminology and Criminal Justice*, 10(1): 11–22.

Kemshall H (2003) *Understanding Risk in Criminal Justice*. Maidenhead: OUP.

Laub JH and Sampson RJ (2003) *Shared Beginnings, Divergent Lives: Delinquent Boys to Age 70*. Cambridge MA: Harvard University Press.

LeBel TP, Burnett R, Maruna S and Bushway S (2008) 'The 'chicken and egg' of subjective and social factors in desistance from crime', *European Journal of Criminology*, 5(2): 131–159.

Lipsey M (1996) 'What do we learn from 400 research studies on the effectiveness of treatment with juvenile delinquents?' in J McGuire (ed) *What Works: Reducing Re-offending*. Chichester: Wiley.

McAra L and McVie S (2010) 'Youth crime and justice: key messages from the Edinburgh Study of Youth Transitions and Crime', *Criminology and Criminal Justice*, 10(20): 179–209.

McNeill F (2004) 'Supporting desistance in probation practice: a response to Maruna, Porter and Carvalho', *Probation Journal*, 51: 241–247.

Maruna S (2001) *Making Good: How Ex-Convicts Reform and Rebuild Their Lives*. Washington DC: American Psychological Association Books.

Massoglia M and Uggen C (2010) 'Settling down and aging out: toward an interactionist theory of desistance and the transition to adulthood', *American Journal of Sociology*, 116(2): 543–582.

Murray C (2010) 'Conceptualizing young people's strategies of resistance to offending as 'active resilience', *British Journal of Social Work*, 40: 115–132.

Murray C (2011) 'Young people's perspectives: the trials and tribulations of going straight', *Criminology and Criminal Justice*, 12(1): 25–40.

Oliver C, Knight A and Candappa M (2006) *Advocacy for Looked-after Children and Children in Need: Achievements and Challenges*. London: Thomas Coram Research Unit.

Pitts J (2001) 'Korrectional Karaoke: New Labour and the zombification of youth justice', *Youth Justice*, 1(2): 3–16.

Pitts J (2003) *The New Politics of Youth Crime*. Basingstoke: Palgrave.

Rutter M (2005) 'Natural experiments, causal influences and policy development', in M Rutter and M Tienda (eds) *Ethnicity and Causal Mechanisms*, New York: Cambridge University Press.

Sampson A and Themelis S (2009) 'Working in the community with young people who offend', *Journal of Youth Studies*, 12(2): 121–137.

Sampson RJ and Laub JH (1993) *Crime in the Making: Pathways and Turning Points through Life*. Cambridge MA: Harvard University Press.

Sampson RJ and Laub JH (2005) 'A life-course view of the development of crime', *ANNALS of the American Academy of Political and Social Science*, 602: 12–45.

Shapland J and Bottoms A (2011) 'Reflections on social values, offending and desistance among young adult recidivists', *Punishment and Society*, 13(3): 256–282.

Skorikov V and Vondracek F (2007) 'Positive career orientation as an inhibitor of adolescent problem behaviour', *Journal of Adolescence*, 30: 131–146.

Smith DJ (2006) *Social Inclusion and Early Desistance from Crime*. Edinburgh Study of Youth Transitions and Crime: Research Digest 12. Edinburgh: Centre for Law and Society.

Stephenson M (2007) *Young People and Offending: Education, Youth Justice and Social Inclusion*. Cullompton: Willan.

Stephenson M, Giller H and Brown S (2011) *Effective Practice in Youth Justice*. Abingdon: Routledge.

Tarling R and Adams M (2012) *Summer Arts Colleges: Digest of the Evaluation Report*. London: Unitas.

Trotter C (1999) *Working with Involuntary Clients*. London: Sage.

Weaver B and McNeill F (2008) 'Desistance', in B Goldson *Dictionary of Youth Justice*. Cullompton: Willan.

West DJ and Farrington OP (1993) *Who Becomes Delinquent?* London: Heinemann.

Whyte B (2009) *Youth Justice in Practice*. Bristol: Policy Press.

5

In practice: translating research into reality

Heidi Dix and Jennifer Meade

Introduction

This chapter describes a process undertaken by 'County' Youth Offending Service (CYOS) to embed effective practice in service delivery. CYOS is a real service but we have chosen to refer to it by a generic name in order to make the process and lessons learnt as generally applicable as possible. It is a youth offending service made up of four field teams, which serves a large county consisting of rural and urban areas with pockets of deprivation. The process of trying to embed effective practice is a work in progress and, given the changing nature of the evidence base, it follows that it always will be. In recognition of the evolving nature of 'effective practice' in youth justice, CYOS has tried to create a framework and culture which increases the likelihood that practitioners will both know about and use the best available evidence of effectiveness in their work with children and young people.

Effective or evidence-based practice?

It might be helpful to start by defining some terms. In CYOS there was considerable debate about whether to use the term 'evidence-based practice' or 'effective practice'. Both had some attractions but neither summed up exactly what we were trying to express. The term 'evidence-based practice' itself has a number of different definitions. Sackett *et al* (1996) describes evidence-based practice as 'the conscientious, explicit and judicious use of current best evidence in making decisions'. This definition covered partly but not wholly what we required. From the start, the aim in CYOS was to maintain a balance between three aspects of practice: professional knowledge; the personal qualities, skills and understanding necessary to be a credible role model; and the actual methods used. 'Effective practice', which the Youth Justice Board (2013a) defines as 'practice which produces the desired outcome' (first defined by Chapman and Hough 1998), was eventually the chosen working term because, although not exact, it seemed the best match available to us. We have however retained the use of the term 'evidence-based' for specific aspects of practice but have deliberately chosen to use a wide definition of what is accepted as evidence. It is likely that we will reconsider the use of this term. Nutley (2003) suggests the use of the term 'evidence informed' (Stewart *et al* 2011: 238) when she discusses the links between research evidence and policy formation, and we think that this probably better suits the use of evidence within CYOS.

Catalysts for change

There were a number of reasons why CYOS believed it was necessary to make some changes to the way it worked with children and young people. An important external catalyst was the publication of the National Audit Office Report *The Youth Justice System in England and Wales: Reducing Offending by Young People* in December 2010. This report found that there was 'little robust information available to youth justice practitioners about which activities or interventions were likely to be effective in reducing offending' (p9). It was published at a time when it was clear that public services faced a future of diminishing resources and achieving value for money would become ever more important. It was therefore of great concern that there was very little good information about where resources should be focused to get the best results.

As well as an external impetus for change, there were also past and current events at play which meant that CYOS was in a place where change was seen to be required but which also made it more possible to achieve change. The last joint inspection report by HMI Probation and other inspectorates had been published in 2004 and the service was found to be 'satisfactory with a good basis for development'. In particular, the report commented on a well led and managed team. This was followed however by a number of changes at leadership level. A number of heads of service came and went, each with different professional backgrounds and slightly different priorities. Each contributed much but inevitably placed a slightly different emphasis on the care versus control continuum.

Washington Irving wrote in the early part of the 19th century that 'there is a certain relief in change, even though it be from bad to worse', but even if one accepts this statement as true, this period of significant instability had some detrimental effects. Staff and managers had come to believe, not unreasonably, that new directions and initiatives were unlikely to be sustained. In fact, CYOS was showing some of the signs of an organisation at risk as defined by the Children's Improvement Board (Hilton 2012). It had symptoms of 'turnover and change in senior leadership; the assumption that performance standards are secure in an atmosphere of service maintenance rather than development; limited self-awareness and no external challenge; and inconsistent observation of practice'.

By 2010, not only was the purpose of the organisation (welfare or risk management) contested by staff and managers, but there was a difference between perceived level of performance and actual performance as evidenced later by case audits. There were no actual systems or processes in place to judge the quality of work, which contributed to some managers overestimating quality and some feeling entirely unclear about how good it was. Indeed there was no clear consensus about 'what good looked like'. A baseline audit and staff interviews carried out in 2011 by external consultants confirmed that there was cause for concern, not just in terms of the quality of case recording (usually the focus of case audit activity), but also in terms of staff understanding of the management of risk and, more especially, of their role in promoting the welfare of children and young people.

The fact that the service was shortly to be re-inspected by HMI Probation was also causing considerable concern. It acted as another external prompt to change. The HMIP inspection criteria indicated that they were interested in how well children and young people had been safeguarded. This helped to shift the emphasis and started to give staff and managers permission to move away from a procedural approach to one in which the importance of relationships became more prominent.

So essentially there were external and internal drivers to change acting on the service. They combined in particular to shine a spotlight on frontline practice. The environment in which the service operated became more favourable to change taking place through a sense of urgency prompted in part by the imminence of an inspection. A rather damning assessment of current practice by the external consultants had contributed to this sense of urgency. At the same time, some pieces of work such as the *Effective Intervention Strategy* (Meade and Dix 2011, revised 2012) were finally completed because, in the light of forthcoming events, they assumed an urgency which they had previously lacked.

In CYOS, preparation for inspection was seized as an opportunity to improve practice on all levels and to help develop a culture of continual organisational development. It allowed the service to assure itself that the basics were right, and to try out and develop techniques which were later applied to the effective practice agenda. For example, the expectations of the inspection itself were interpreted to staff in a way which was intended to appeal to them and chime with their motivation. In addition, the process of improvement emphasised and built on the strengths that individual practitioners already had. By focusing on strengths and challenging key behaviours, it adopted the first step recommended in Katzenbach *et al* (2012) in *Culture Change That Sticks*. It also provided common standards and language and a shared understanding of 'what good looked like' which provided a solid foundation for later developments and was the first important step in starting to build a culture of high expectations within the service.

At about the same time, Coalition Government cuts to funding of local authorities prompted reorganisation of children's services in the county and CYOS was not immune. It was reorganised with redundancies, changes to the structure of the senior management team and modifications to team structures including the creation of a new operational team. The process of reorganisation and the anxiety amongst staff groups had the potential to derail the improvement programme and did result in a temporary reduction in focus. Our progress in embedding this agenda has been variable and there is no doubt that it has been negatively affected and sometimes seems in danger of being derailed by the present challenging financial and political environment.

The starting point

In terms of the promotion and embedding of the effective practice agenda, on reflection, we were working from a number of implicit beliefs. In brief, these were the importance of a blend of skills, knowledge and experience which practitioners brought to their work with young people, including the central but neglected importance of the relationship between the young person and the practitioner These form the context in which interventions are delivered and change takes place (see Figure 5.1). We were also concerned with the distance between strategy and practice, which was often observed in initiatives within the service and elsewhere, and wanted to avoid this in the work we did by, as far as possible, taking a non-hierarchical approach. The *Asset* assessment system has been criticised for the deficit model it employs, and this deficit model sometimes seemed to have seeped into other aspects of policy and practice within the service. We wanted to turn this on its head and take a strengths-based approach. We wanted to find a way of retaining real creativity at the same time as minimising practice developed mainly with the skills and interests of the worker in mind. Peters and Waterman (1982) suggest that shared values are at the heart of a functioning organisation, and therefore effective communication of the commitment to effective practice was essential. Within the service, the overall aim was to promote a culture of learning (Senge 1990) that is based on mutual trust and openness where staff members are encouraged to become reflective practitioners (Schön 1983). CYOS is attempting to become a 'reflective organisation' and has decided to use this definition instead of that of 'learning organisation' due to the association with managerialism that the latter carries (Ruch 2012).

Figure 5.1:
Relationship-based
practice

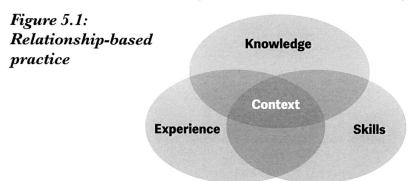

Firstly perhaps it's helpful to explain how we had arrived at the view that the relationship-based aspects of the effective practice agenda were in danger of being marginalised. At a CYOS service day at the start of the new millennium, a representative of the Youth Justice Board (YJB) spoke about the ethos behind the development and design of the newly created multi-agency youth offending teams. He explained that the strength of these teams was that they provided a 'one-stop shop' for young people who would attend appointments with a range of professionals such as education and health workers who would be able to meet their individual needs. He was asked by the audience how he felt this model was likely to affect relationships between young people and their case manager. His reply was dismissive: he described relationship-based practice as 'old hat'.

This statement caused consternation in much of his audience. Some had seen in practice the result of such an approach in different settings; for example the probation service, which had invested heavily in evidence-based, accredited groupwork programmes, had started to see high attrition rates and somewhat belatedly started to rediscover the vital role of a central relationship between worker and client which they described as 'case management'.

In addition, many had come from professions that held, as an article of faith, the idea that the ability to develop and sustain relationships with children, young people and their families was key to achieving positive outcomes (Ruch *et al* 2010, Munro 2011). Therefore the perspective the Youth Justice Board was taking at the time was felt to be, at best, short-sighted by at least some of their audience.

Defining the effective practitioner

Again, perhaps it is helpful at this point to go into a bit more detail about terms. We have already mentioned but not fully described a blend of factors which we variously called relationship-based practice, case management and other terms, none of which seemed exactly right. When we explored these factors, we realised that we were describing a combination of: the behaviours, values and personal qualities of the worker; the professional knowledge base, reflection and curiosity to learn more which they brought to the work; and how and what they actually delivered. (It is, after all, perfectly possible to have a professional relationship with a young person or any other service user without the intention or likelihood of promoting positive change.) One of our first concerns therefore was to define in more detail what research indicated was the precise nature of an effective working relationship between practitioner and young person, and what skills practitioners needed to build such relationships. Drawing heavily on the work of McNeill *et al* (2005), Holt (2000) and Davies (2006), these skills were summarised in the *Effective Intervention Strategy* (Meade and Dix 2012) as the ability to display empathy, respect and warmth, to establish a 'working alliance' (a mutual understanding and agreement about the nature and purpose of intervention), and to adopt an approach that is person-centred, collaborative and client-driven. Much has been written about behaviour, values and personal qualities as aspects of effective practice. For example, Newman *et al* (2005) talk about the importance of forming a trusting and mutually respectful relationship with the emphasis on young people being active participants rather than passive in a process of change. The National Youth Agency in 2010 commented on the importance of agreed goals, and Miller and Rollnick (2013) on the importance of negotiation and agreement of tasks in achieving desired outcomes – all of which is especially important in an involuntary setting such as youth justice.

Embedding effective practice

If you want to move people, it has to be toward a vision that is positive for them.

(Martin Luther King)

Fundamental to the development of a culture of effective practice is the need to develop the curiosity and interest of practitioners. It is important that staff feel able to take risks, to be creative and to learn from situations if they do not go as planned, with the appropriate facilitation and support from managers (Hudson 2007).

With this in mind, a number of approaches were taken within the service to develop the inquisitiveness of practitioners. These initiatives are outlined in more detail below.

The effective practice group

The effective practice group is made up of a cross-grade group of staff and includes a member of the senior management team, an operational manager, senior officers and at least one practitioner from each team. Practitioners from the group act as 'champions' of effective practice within their teams; their role is to inspire effective practice and 'research mindedness' in terms of developing and selecting interventions for use with children and young people. They act as a resource within their teams and share evidence that exists or is emerging within youth justice. The group as a whole takes responsibility for which interventions can be included as part of the CYOS effective intervention preferred list.

The preferred list allows practitioners to be confident that any interventions they choose from this list have been based upon principles of effective practice. An extract from the preferred list can be seen below.

Area for intervention	Resource
Parenting	Parent Talk (available in the West team)
	Triple P
Social skills	Why Try? (available in the South team)
	Boyhood 2 Manhood (available in the North team)
	Female Group (available in the South and West teams)
	Only Girls Allowed (available in the North team)
	The Duke of Edinburgh's Award (all teams)
	Teen Talk

In order to achieve a balance between the freedom to innovate and the development of evidence-based interventions and programmes, the following process is used (see Figure 5.2):

 ▶ A practitioner has an idea to develop a programme or intervention

 ▶ The programme designer uses the Youth Justice Board *Programme*

Development Toolkit (2013b) to help create or benchmark their innovation

▶ The practitioner presents their programme to the effective practice group using the YJB *Programme Development Toolkit* as a template

▶ Approval is given by the effective practice group if there is a sufficient evidence base for the programme for it to be used within the service. Alternatively, recommendations or suggestions are given by the group and support is provided to develop the programme to ensure it has a sufficient evidence base; the revised version is presented to the group at a later date

▶ A nationally recognised accreditation is awarded by the learning development co-ordinator

▶ The programme or intervention is adopted onto the effective intervention preferred list.

Figure 5.2: The innovation process

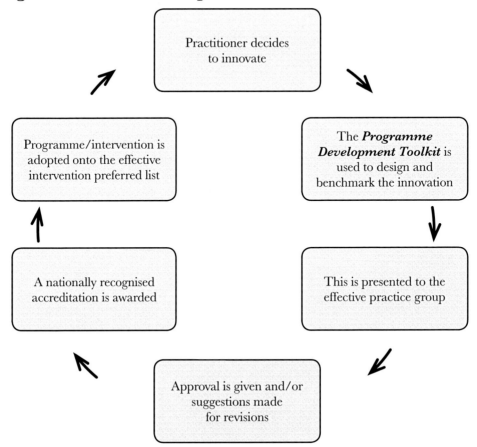

A description of a locally designed programme that is included in the effective intervention preferred list can be seen below.

Resource	Description	Preferred list status
Boyhood 2 Manhood	A groupwork programme that works on both static and dynamic factors in young men's lives and challenges both entrenched views and peer-led beliefs. Suitable for: ▸ All learning styles ▸ Ages 12–18 ▸ Any intervention level ▸ Particularly suitable for young men who lack a positive role model Ongoing rolling programme. Available in the North team.	Programme developed locally. Benchmark completed. Preferred programme.

An example of how this process might work in practice is illustrated below in a case study.

> ### Case study: Sally
>
> Sally had been working with a number of young men who required intervention in relation to their identity and the beliefs that they held about themselves and other people. Sally felt this was influencing the way they were thinking and behaving, and she believed it was a big part of the reason why they were involved in criminal behaviour.
>
> She had been exploring with her manager the possibility of devising a groupwork intervention which would cover these areas. Her manager advised her to look on both CYOS's effective intervention preferred list and in the YJB's effective practice library to see if they contained anything that could assist her. Sally did this but was not able to find a resource that seemed to deliver exactly what she needed, so she decided to devise a new programme. She spoke to a member of her team, James, who she knew was involved in the effective practice group. He explained that effective programmes for young people tended to be those that matched the level of risk posed by the child or young person and that focused on targeting factors that can be changed by using a skills-based approach. Sally was already aware that the content of her programme

and any activities or exercises she was using needed to meet a range of diverse needs and different learning styles.

James advised Sally to consider taking a cognitive behavioural approach to explore issues of identity, thinking and behaviour with the intervention participants as these seemed to be the areas highlighted within the assessment. He suggested that Sally could also explore moral reasoning with the participants. He explained that these approaches have been demonstrated to be effective in addressing specific forms of antisocial attitudes or values which may contribute to criminal behaviour in young men. Sally did some background reading and learnt that moral reasoning training exposes individuals to a range of moral dilemmas though discussion and decision-making exercises. She liked the idea of this as she could use a range of material that would be relevant and meaningful to participants.

She decided that the intervention group would meet once a week for six weeks in a local youth centre and that each session would last for approximately one hour. She was aware of the need to consider her behaviour and communication skills as she was the group facilitator, and to make sure that she was prompt as this was part of the two-way agreement that participants had previously signed. She was also aware from her personal reading that modelling positive behaviours and attitudes is important when working with children and young people (Trotter 2009). Sally had a youth work background and so was aware of the need to establish a positive rapport with young people in order to effect change, and so proposed meeting individual participants with their case manager prior to the group commencing.

Once Sally had used the YJB *Programme Development Toolkit* to assist the development of her programme, she presented her proposal to the effective practice group. The group considered the evidence base underpinning the content of Sally's programme and found that she had not really considered how she would measure the effectiveness of her intervention programme on participants. The group recommended that Sally ask participants to complete a short questionnaire both before and after the programme to see if any changes had occurred in their thinking and attitudes. The effective practice group also suggested that participants be tracked both six and 12 months after the intervention had finished to see if they had committed any further offences. Sally agreed to do this with the support of the performance management team.

The effective practice group also asked Sally to consider how she would involve the case manager, education services and the families of participants in the programme, as this would help to reinforce participants' knowledge and allow them to practise any skills they may have learnt. As a result, Sally decided to prepare a presentation about the programme and deliver this at the next team meeting. She also added an additional session to which case managers, family members and key education providers were invited, to showcase the work that had been undertaken by the participants. Sally introduced feedback sheets and regular three-way meetings with case managers to ensure that they were able to support and extend learning which had taken place in the intervention group on an individual basis. She arranged to talk to individual case managers about how they could support attendance and learning.

The effective practice group also questioned Sally about how her intervention would link to other aspects of the young person's intervention plan such as access to education, training or employment, or support to integrate within the wider community. They made the point that work with individual young people and their families was important but she should also remain aware of the need to address wider structural issues.

Sally assured the effective practice group that case managers would be working on these aspects and that she had chosen to run the programme in local, open-access youth provision so that participants could be introduced to the provision. (The provision was used by a variety of young people who were not involved in offending.) It was hoped that, by introducing this mainstream resource to participants, they would continue to use this provision outside of their appointments with CYOS.

Sally then met with the learning development co-ordinator to investigate the most appropriate accreditation that would be awarded to participants when they had completed the programme. Sally's intervention was then added to the preferred list of effective interventions used within the service. Sally gave presentations in team meetings across the service, as well as to magistrates and panel members, to inform them about her innovative programme.

How much is enough?

Please, sir, I want some more.

(Charles Dickens)

In deciding which programmes and interventions were accepted onto the preferred list, the issue of what would be accepted as sufficient evidence had to be considered. When initially researching evidence-based practice within the youth justice sector, the focus was on interventions that had been subject to the most robust testing, ie through the use of gold-standard research methods such as randomised control trials and systematic reviews. However, we quickly realised that, in practice, this was likely to stifle home-grown innovation as it would be impossible to replicate such methods locally. We needed to reconsider what we would accept as credible evidence both because programmes and interventions based on robust evidence were limited, and because we did not wish to stifle creativity within the service. CYOS did however purchase some rigorously evaluated programmes such as the Triple P parenting programme, as well as supporting Multidimensional Treatment Foster Care and providing training to staff on these interventions.

As part of our critical appraisal and in line with the recommendations of the National Audit Office (2010), CYOS decided to source programmes that did not carry a body of 'hardcore' evidence behind them but that did appear to have credible evidence 'designed into them'. By this we mean programmes that seemed to have common elements of effective practice built into them, including components such as cognitive behavioural techniques and strengths-based approaches. We requested details of the evidence the programme designers had used to design their resources, which we reviewed; we then purchased the programme if we were satisfied with the evidence that was provided. In deciding whether to buy in a programme, we were also influenced by internal CYOS asset analysis and selected programmes which targeted areas of high need identified in the analysis.

In terms of home-grown programmes, the approach has already been described but is based again on the National Audit Office principles of benchmarking interventions against the 'common elements' of effective programmes (Edovald 2013) and trying to design effectiveness into new interventions. We accept that this will not produce a product with a gold-standard evidence base but believe that, since the role of practitioners is so crucial in effecting positive change, overall CYOS stands a better chance of achieving positive outcomes for children and young people with well motivated and positive staff.

Team effective practice budgets

Kotter (1990) suggested that rewards and the recognition of progress and achievements are essential for successful change. With this in mind, each member of the effective practice group was allocated a small budget and, in return, asked to demonstrate how they would use this to contribute to the development of evidence-based practice within their team.

Dealing with resistance

One of the first things that was done in CYOS was to commission bespoke motivational interviewing training across the service to assist practitioners with the proactive engagement of children, young people and their families. As well as investing in this training, the principles of this approach (Miller and Rollnick 2002) were used to deal with the resistance that was encountered from some staff. Techniques such as expressing empathy towards the pressures that staff were feeling in relation to the imminent inspection, together with 'rolling with resistance' (Miller and Rollnick 2002: 40) were utilised. By actively involving practitioners in finding answers and solutions to develop a culture of effective practice within the service, resistance was reduced. Anxieties were dealt with by demonstrating that what was required of staff could be achieved and providing the necessary mechanisms to achieve it. The facilitation of self-belief together with the nurturing of a sense of personal responsibility, in addition to the techniques listed above, provided the necessary conditions for cultural change.

In order to achieve the learning culture we wished to create, we were mindful of the need to pay attention to the individual personality types and learning styles of people within the service. In recognition of this, various mechanisms were used to help embed change. These are explained in the following sections.

Performance management and supervision

Everybody has different needs that depend on a range of factors including skills, knowledge, confidence, gender, ethnicity and culture. Some practitioners may require more nurturing than others, depending on personality types and whether they are operating from a secure base (Bowlby 1988). Rogers (2002) suggests that learning is affected by the personality type of an individual; whether somebody is an introvert or an extrovert affects how receptive they are to change. Therefore, within supervision, it was necessary to help individual practitioners to identify skills and experience they could bring to the change process to build confidence. Managers were encouraged to use pro-social modelling techniques (Bandura 1977) to lead practitioners through the change process. The commitment to an effective practice agenda was reflected in the service's performance development framework where all grades within the service were asked to evidence their contribution to the implementation of the effective intervention strategy.

Hawkins and Shohet (2000) suggest that supervision is an ideal place for an organisation to learn, develop and culturally evolve, and that there is a need to provide processes for discussions and dialogue that occur within supervision to be shared with the wider organisation. The creative and innovative ideas that are developed within supervision are shared at CYOS through practice development sessions.

Practice development sessions

Research suggests that practitioners build their knowledge and skills not only through formal training opportunities and the application of policy and procedures, but also through opportunities to think through the actions, practice and work they have undertaken, ie 'reflective practice' (Schön 1983). Clearly supervision provides opportunities for this to take place on an individual basis with practitioners, but staff at CYOS stated that they would also value the opportunity to discuss and reflect upon their practice with colleagues.

In response to this, practice development sessions were created. They occur monthly across the service and are often led by practitioners within the teams. They generally last for two hours and it is an expectation that all practitioners and managers attend each session. The content of these sessions is also informed by findings from the internal audit/performance management as well as the developing effective practice agenda.

Direct work observations

Observations of direct work carried out by practitioners has long been a feature of education and training within services such as social work. In recent years there has been a move to extend this beyond initial training and continue the observation of staff undertaking direct work as part of continuing professional development. We decided to adopt this approach within CYOS as this was one of the few ways we could find to gain evidence about and directly influence the quality of the professional interaction between children and young people and their practitioners. It was also an opportunity to ensure that direct work with children, young people and their families was informed by evidence-based interventions. A key component was the use of a 'feedback wheel' (Suffolk County Council 2010) (see Figure 5.3 opposite) to gain the perspective of the young person, and this was used to inform the overall learning of the staff member who was being observed.

As a way to share and promote an evidence-based way of working, we are also hoping to include peer reviews of practice (Shardlow and Doel 1996) where practitioners will have opportunities to undertake observations of each other and offer feedback.

Figure 5.3: The feedback wheel

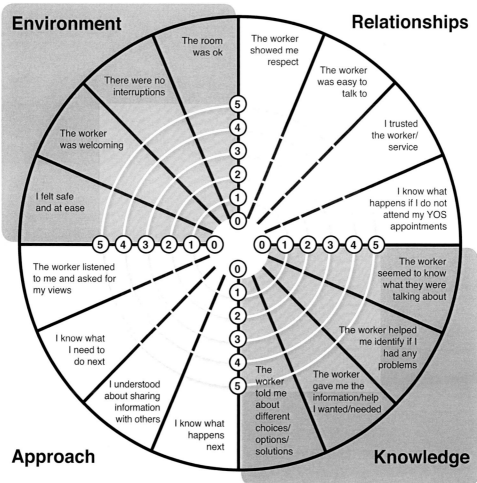

We would like your opinion on the service that you have received.

Please put a cross on the circle which describes how you feel:

5 = I **strongly** agree with the statement and am **very** happy with what the worker did.

4 = I agree with the statement and am happy with what the worker did.

3 = I am unsure.

2 = I disagree with the statement and am unhappy with what the worker did.

1 = I **strongly** disagree with the statement and am **very** unhappy with what the worker did.

0 = Not applicable.

Are there any other comments, you want to make?

Please write them on the back of this sheet.

What happens now?

The manager looks at your form along with others and then talk to the worker.

If you have marked low scores, would you be willing for a manager to talk to you to help improve the service? If so please put your name and telephone number on the back of this sheet.

Thanks for your help

Practice Matters

Involvement and communication in the change process is vital for co-operation and support. Failing to communicate effectively with people can arouse suspicion and create both defensiveness and resistance. With this in mind, an in-house newsletter provided another method to communicate the vision of the service. It consistently included items that promoted the effective practice agenda within the service. A themed edition was also produced entitled *Effective Practice Matters!* with many members of the service contributing articles. These included personal testimonies regarding the use of the Youth Justice Board *Programme Development Toolkit* (YJB 2013b) and how the *Effective Intervention Strategy* (Meade and Dix 2012) informed one practitioner's approach. It was also used to publicise a celebration event that was held within the service.

Effective practice event

Rogers (2002) suggests that there are two types of motivation – intrinsic motivation and extrinsic motivation – and suggests that intrinsic motivational factors are generally stronger then extrinsic ones. However, Miller and Rollnick (2002) argue that motivation is not always present in an individual and is something that can be influenced by interpersonal interactions. Therefore, an all-staff day was planned to celebrate the positive work and to recognise the innovation that was apparent within the service. The event also helped to promote the effective intervention strategy, showcased effective practice from around the county in the form of seminars presented by managers and practitioners, and provided opportunities for shared learning.

Young people also contributed to the day and presented the findings from recent focus groups that had taken place across the service.

Partnership with local university

In partnership with the local university, CYOS has also commissioned what we have described as a 'scoping' exercise. This will explore, through case studies and interviews with a cross-section of staff, how staff actually make decisions about what approaches and interventions they use with particular children and young people, as well as looking in depth into how information actually disseminates around the service. This information will be used to inform our future approaches.

CYOS has also commissioned the production of an easily applied outcome measurement tool which can be used with groupwork and with individual interventions.

Future directions

At CYOS, we are also interested in how we can involve children and young people more fully in the development of the effective practice agenda. The youth justice system has been criticised (National Youth Agency 2010, 2011) for not doing enough to ensure the active participation of young people, and there has been some debate about the appropriateness of considering young people's opinions of the services they use in a youth justice context. It has been suggested that their involvement is at best difficult, at worst inappropriate, when young people receive intervention on a non-voluntary basis as part of a court-ordered sentence.

Article 12 of the United Nations *Convention on the Rights of the Child* (UNCRC) (United Nations 1989) clearly outlines the right that young people have to be heard in decisions that affect them, and although the UNCRC is not part of the legislative framework in our country, the need to consider the wishes and feelings of a child is contained within the Children Act 2004 (HM Government 2004). The active participation of young people and their families in the design and delivery of interventions or individual support plans, and the shaping of services, is an important component in achieving a reduction in offending (National Youth Agency 2011). In the future, CYOS hopes to explore ways in which young people can become co-researchers in the evaluation of practice (McLaughlin 2009).

The IDEA approach to case management

As mentioned earlier, facilitating the development of the mix of skills, knowledge and experience (see Figure 5.1) necessary to be an effective practitioner was at the heart of the change that was needed within CYOS. As part of our commitment to this, we identified an approach to case management that we call the IDEA model (see Figure 5.4 overleaf). This is comprised of the following four elements:

▶ **Influence**. This element is about the appropriate use by the practitioner of their personal qualities to bring about positive change. It is about values, motivation and behaviour and, in our opinion, is the part of the picture that tends to be most neglected in practice. Practitioners must be able to act as appropriate role models and understand the impact they may have in doing so. We have called this appropriate use of 'moral authority' influence.

▶ **Delivery**. This element includes the professional skills that are necessary to deliver accurate and meaningful assessments, focused and achievable plans, and meaningful interventions. However, it also includes the ability to co-ordinate, review and amend any or all of these in the light of change or new information. Delivery is focused on how these processes are undertaken and is underpinned by the ability to engage young people, parents/carers, partners and victims.

▶ **Expertise**. This element consists of the professional knowledge and awareness of research that is necessary in order to select the most effective approaches, interventions and programmes. A commitment to critically reflect on and learn from experience is also essential to develop professional expertise.

▶ **Alliance**. Finally, practitioners must have effective engagement skills. Fundamental to this is the ability to develop an alliance based on empathy, respect and warmth, as well as adopting an approach that is person-centred, collaborative and client-driven (McNeill *et al* 2005). Criticisms of evidence-based practice suggest that it is too prescribed, with a 'doing to' rather than a 'doing with' approach' (Newman *et al* 2005: 117) and therefore a relationship that is based on mutual respect is important.

Figure 5.4: The IDEA approach to case management

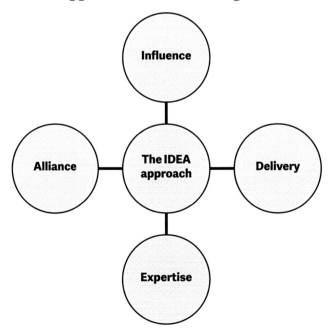

Reflections and lessons learnt

The future's so bright, I gotta wear shades.

(Timbuk3)

County Youth Offending Service began embedding effective practice in a context which was influenced by a number of factors. There were strong external circumstances which created a sense that a change in approach was imminently required. At the same time, internal factors such as the commitment of key management staff created an environment in which permission was given to start the work.

The service had already embarked on a programme to improve all aspects of service delivery, and this programme both supported and underpinned the effective practice agenda by ensuring that the basics were right. It also contributed significantly to starting to create a cultural change in which high professional expectations were normal. Last but not least, it introduced structures and processes which held the realities of practice up to the light and enabled staff at all levels of the organisation to recognise the need for change and to own and promote it.

CYOS's *Effective Intervention Strategy* (Meade and Dix 2012) stated clearly that 'the context in which intervention is delivered and the skills of the practitioner in effective delivery are at least as important as what programme is delivered'. The service also refused to allow the wider relationship-based aspects to be deleted from the picture. In our opinion, this proved vital in moving the effective practice agenda forward as it meant that the aspects of the work that staff held most dear were clearly part of the agenda and not irrelevant to it. As part of this process, practitioners and managers have had the way they have always done things questioned. Some have found this very challenging. Long-held beliefs have been put under the spotlight and sometimes found wanting. We have attempted to use this challenge positively in the ways already described, but some staff still struggle. It would be quite wrong to say that this initiative commands universal support but the pockets of enthusiasm for it within the organisation are definitely growing.

Since CYOS started on this journey, some aspects of the approach we have taken have been mirrored by developments within the Youth Justice Board – on the classification of programmes and interventions, for example. Where we believe our work remains different is in its emphasis on a holistic method. We also believe that the process of internal review carried out by the effective practice group has in itself proved helpful in developing the knowledge of the practitioners that attend it on a regular basis and those who come to present to it. There has been excellent feedback about how presenting interventions to the group has made practitioners consider other aspects and so helped to make the end product likely to be more effective. Even if there is now an element of duplication, we would be reluctant to lose our internal process.

In order for cultural change to have longevity, Kotter (1990) suggests that it needs to be woven into the organisation. This is what we have attempted to do in CYOS. It has been a process, rather like desistance from offending, characterised by ambivalence and uncertainty. We are struck, on reflection, by the complex process of negotiation and compromise, meshing and balancing that has had to take place in order to make any headway at all. The difficulties of finding the right definitions to describe what we wanted to express are an illustration of the struggle to try and adapt theory to practice in the real world of service delivery. It is also perhaps worth acknowledging that this work has been undertaken against the backdrop of a particularly challenging environment in local government.

Practitioners need to not feel constrained by a culture of evidence-based practice, but rather feel inspired and supported to develop their critical thinking and reflective abilities. Encouragement is needed for practitioners and managers to become curious about what works effectively with children, young people and their families. A strengths-based approach was taken across CYOS, with practitioners being supported by members of the effective practice group to build on what they are doing well and to link this to research and evidence. We have found balancing performance and the management of cases with space for reflection in supervision a challenge, and one of our next major pieces of work will be to work on a solution to this.

A service that is truly based on the principles of effective practice requires a commitment across all levels, with practitioners, managers and senior managers each playing their role. These roles and responsibilities can be defined as follows:

Practitioners should:

- Assess cases accurately and ensure that this assessment leads to the right risk classification so that the right offending-related factors are addressed and the right level of intervention is delivered

- Plan interventions and programmes carefully, taking into account engagement skills and approaches that are based on effective practice principles

▶ Ensure that the planned programme of intervention is delivered

▶ Review assessments in the light of new information and amend interventions in the light of that review if required

▶ Think about how changes achieved will be sustained after contact finishes and plan this in from the beginning

▶ Keep up to date with relevant research and new resources

▶ As the effective intervention preferred list is developed, choose intervention material from it

▶ Develop new programmes and interventions, taking into account existing information on effectiveness

▶ Benchmark any interventions they develop.

Managers should:

▶ Focus on the quality of planning and intervention delivery in supervision

▶ Complete direct work observations annually on all staff they supervise

▶ Ensure new programmes and interventions are submitted to the effective practice group for inclusion on the preferred list

▶ Support staff to benchmark programmes

▶ Support the delivery of groupwork programmes in all areas through the flexible use of staff

▶ Support staff to keep up to date with relevant research and resources

▶ Deliver supervision that has a reflective component.

The service should:

▶ Develop a systematic, consistent process to collect feedback from groupwork and other interventions and ensure this is analysed and the results acted upon

▶ Ensure preferred interventions and programmes are available across the county

▶ Support the professional development of staff in order to enable them to deliver this strategy

▶ Ensure resources are available to support the delivery of this strategy

▶ Analyse assessments regularly to determine what areas of offending-related need are most prevalent on the CYOS caseload and ensure resources are available to address these.

In order for practitioners to become research-aware and to develop critical thinking skills, managers need to be able to facilitate their learning and organisational support needs to be provided at a senior managerial level. In essence the system – in this instance the service – needs to be ready and able to implement this way of working (Edovald 2013).

In summary, we would suggest that evidence-based practice is not a substitute for practice wisdom or for the dismissal of the voice of children and young people (Newman *et al* 2005). Rather, it is by merging these approaches that exciting possibilities are to be found that can provide positive outcomes for children, young people and their families.

References

Bandura A (1977) *Social Learning Theory*. New York: General Learning Press.

Bowlby J (1988) *A Secure Base*. Oxon: Routledge.

Chapman T and Hough M (1998) *Evidence Based Practice: A Guide to Effective Practice*. London: Home Office.

Davies K (2006) 'Case management and Think First completion', *Probation Journal*, 53(3): 213–229. London: Sage.

Edovald T (2013) *What is Evidence-based Practice?* Social Research Unit Webinar, 03/04/13.

Hawkins P and Shohet R (2000) *Supervision in the Helping Professions* (2nd edn). Buckingham: Open University Press.

Hilton C (2012) *Indicators of Organisational Risk*. Children's Improvement Board.

Holt P (2000) *Case Management: Context for Supervision: Community and Criminal Justice. Monograph 2*. Leicester: De Montfort University.

HM Government (2004) *The Children Act*. London: The Stationery Office.

HM Inspectorate of Probation (HMIP) (2004) *Joint Inspection Report of Youth Offending Teams of England and Wales. Report on: Suffolk Youth Offending Service*. London: The Stationery Office.

Hudson M (2007) 'Managing people', in Harrison R, Benjamin C, Curran S and Hunter R *Leading Work With Young People*. Milton Keynes: The Open University/London: Sage.

Katzenbach JR, Steffen I and Kronley C (2012) 'Cultural Change That Sticks', *Harvard Business Review*, 90. New York: Harvard Business Publishing.

Kotter JP (1990) *A Force for Change: How Leadership Differs from Management*. New York: Free Press.

McLaughlin H (2009) *Service User Research in Health and Social Care*. London: Sage.

McNeill F, Batchelor S, Burnett R and Knox J (2005) *Reducing Re-offending: Key Practice Skills*. Edinburgh: Scottish Social Work Inspection Agency.

Meade J and Dix H (2012) *Effective Intervention Strategy*. Suffolk: Suffolk Youth Offending Service [unpublished].

Miller WR and Rollnick S (2002) *Motivational Interviewing: Preparing People for Change* (2nd edn). New York: Guilford Press.

Miller WR and Rollnick S (2013) *Motivational Interviewing: Helping People Change* (3rd edn). New York: Guilford Press.

Munro E (2011) *The Munro Review of Child Protection: Final Report. A Child-centred System*. London: The Stationery Office.

National Audit Office (2010) *The Youth Justice System in England and Wales: Reducing Offending by Young People*. London: The Stationery Office.

National Youth Agency (2010) *Voice and Influence in the Youth Justice System*. Leicester: Local Government Association.

National Youth Agency (2011) *Participation in Youth Justice: Measuring Impact and Effectiveness*. Leicester: Local Government Association.

Newman T, Moseley A, Tierney S and Ellis A (2005) *Evidence-based Social Work: A Guide for the Perplexed*. Dorset: Russell House Publishing.

Nutley S (2003) 'Bridging the policy/research divide: reflections and lessons from the United Kingdom', in Stewart A, Allard T and Dennison S (2011) *Evidence-based Policy and Practice in Youth Justice*. Sydney: The Federation Press.

Peters TJ and Waterman RH (1982) *In Search of Excellence*. New York: Harper & Row.

Rogers A (2002) *Teaching Adults*. Maidenhead: Open University Press.

Ruch G, Turney D and Ward A (2010) *Relationship-based Social Work: Getting to the Heart of Practice*. London: Jessica Kingsley.

Ruch G (2012) 'Where have all the feelings gone? Developing reflective and relationship-based management in child-care social work', *British Journal of Social Work*, 42(7): 1315–1332.

Sackett DL, Rosenberg WM, Gray JA, Haynes RB and Richardson WS (1996) 'Evidence-based medicine: what it is and what it isn't', *British Medical Journal*, 312(7023): 71–2.

Schön D (1983) *The Reflective Practitioner: How Professionals Think in Action.* London: Temple Smith.

Senge PM (1990) *The Fifth Discipline: The Art and Practice of the Learning Organization.* London: Random House.

Shardlow S and Doel M (1996) *Practice Learning and Teaching.* Basingstoke: Macmillan/BASW.

Suffolk County Council (2010) *The Feedback Wheel.* Suffolk: Suffolk Youth Support Service [unpublished].

Trotter C (2009) 'Pro-social modelling', *European Journal of Probation*, 1(2): 142–152.

United Nations (1989) *Convention on the Rights of the Child.* New York: United Nations.

Whittaker A (2009) *Research Skills for Social Work.* Exeter: Learning Matters.

Youth Justice Board (2013a) *Innovation and Evaluation in Youth Justice: Guidance and Resources.* London: The Stationery Office.

Youth Justice Board (2013b) *Programme Development Toolkit.* London: The Stationery Office.